Atrium

Atrium

Charles Rice

The MIT Press
Cambridge, Massachusetts
London, England

The MIT Press would like to thank the anonymous peer reviewers who provided comments on drafts of this book. The generous work of academic experts is essential for establishing the authority and quality of our publications. We acknowledge with gratitude the contributions of these otherwise uncredited readers.

This book was set in Bembo Book MT Pro by New Best-set Typesetters Ltd. Printed and bound in the United States of America.

Library of Congress Cataloging-in-Publication Data

Names: Rice, Charles, author.
Title: Atrium / Charles Rice.
Description: Cambridge, Massachusetts : The MIT Press, [2023] | Includes bibliographical references and index.
Identifiers: LCCN 2022050529 | ISBN 9780262048330 (hardcover)
Subjects: LCSH: Atrium buildings. | Architecture and society—History—20th century.
Classification: LCC NA4160 .R525 2023 | DDC 720/.48—dc23/eng/20221109
LC record available at https://lccn.loc.gov/2022050529

10 9 8 7 6 5 4 3 2 1

Contents

List of Images

Prologue: The Generic Building Form of the Late Twentieth Century

On 16 June 2015, a presidential candidacy was declared. The event occurred not on the steps of a state capitol, nor on a hastily erected platform in a town square, nor even under the hot lights of a television studio. Rather, in the atrium of a mixed-use tower in Midtown Manhattan, the candidate took a short escalator ride from an upper-level gallery down to the waiting media below. What looked like an attempt to grab headlines gathered an extreme kind of momentum, the candidate riding a wave of political disruption all the way to the White House.

Looking back at this event, which seems like an age ago, what is remarkable is that it took place in a space that itself seemed to belong to another time, and another presidency. As the quintessential space of market-led developmentalism, Trump Tower (Swanke Hayden Connell, 1983) symbolized a kind of architecture that became ascendant with the neoliberal conservatism of Ronald Reagan. The setting, then, was perhaps not so incongruous; by 2015, an escalator ride through a marble-and-mirror atrium was staged as a triumphal entrance.

An escalator ride also emblematized the way in which such privatized, commercial spaces were received in architectural criticism in the aftermath of Reagan's presidency. The cover of Michael Sorkin's edited collection

Figure 0.1 Trump Tower, New York. Swanke Hayden Connell Architects, 1983. RIBA Collections.

Variations on a Theme Park: The New American City and the End of Public Space, published in 1992, featured an image of five classically robed figures (three men ahead, two women following) peering about themselves, bewildered, as they were carried down by escalator into the gleaming core of what we assume to be a shopping mall. Something had diverted them on the way to the agora. The appearance of such incongruous figures in the mall spoke volumes about the concepts of place, public and politics that underpinned the book, and what its target were: classical, universally understood values of the authentic city were under siege from a banal, consumer-driven uniformity that was both everywhere and nowhere. A concept and experience of the city defined in terms of publicness, presence, and propinquity was being replaced by that of an ersatz, placeless, decentered city. Where once the city had provided an architectural legibility regarding hierarchy and order, in its dissolution "anything seems to go with anything—hierarchies are both reinforced and concealed, at once fixed and despatialized."[1] While shopping malls, themed leisure environments, and segregated developments were the main examples Sorkin and his contributors used to describe this new urban reality, the atrium, in its most popular and visible form of the atrium hotel, crystalized the condition: "it can be inserted equally in an open field or in the heart of town; the inward-looking atrium hotel is as apt to the featureless greensward as it is to the teeming unreclaimed downtowns."[2] A quarter of a century later, a presidential candidacy declared in an atrium could readily be seen as the culmination of the politics of this new American city and its voided public space. Yet the candidate might have nodded knowingly at these robed visitors. In Athens, seemingly the ideal city, political participation had been restricted: one had to be male and a citizen.

Notwithstanding Sorkin's idealism regarding political participation,[3] the problem the atrium was seen to present was not its ersatz quality but the perception that it supplanted architecture's exterior presence. As Fredric Jameson surmised after walking through the atrium of John Portman's Bonaventure Hotel in Los Angeles (1977) in the mid-1980s, "it does not

Figure 0.2 Bonaventure Hotel, Los Angeles. John Portman & Associates, 1977. © 1977 Alexandre Georges. Courtesy The Portman Archives.

wish to be a part of the city but rather its equivalent and replacement or substitute."[4] The atrium was a threat to architecture's symbolic power and the way in which it ordered—and drew order from—the urban realm around it. Jameson saw that the self-sufficient interior urbanism of the Bonaventure's atrium had "been imposed by some new category of enclosure governing the inner space of the hotel itself."[5] To locate oneself within the atrium and understand its extent, "the language of volume or volumes"[6] seemed inadequate. The escalator ride again had a significant role to play in what was at stake in this new kind of space: "the escalators and elevators here henceforth replace movement but also, and above all, designate themselves as new reflexive signs and emblems of movement proper. . . . Here, the narrative stroll has been underscored, symbolized, reified, and replaced by a transportation machine which becomes the allegorical signifier of that older promenade we are no longer allowed to conduct on our own."[7]

Jameson took up the concept of the cognitive map to attempt to bridge between this bewildering spatial experience and what he called late capitalism's "great, global multinational and decentered communicational network in which we find ourselves caught as individual subjects."[8] In his 1960 book *The Image of the City*, urbanist Kevin Lynch had developed the concept of the cognitive map to describe how urban space became legible and therefore memorable for a city's inhabitants. Jameson adopted the concept in order to show its limits with respect to a space such as the atrium. The vast interior materialized an illegibility, and it held, negatively, an explanatory power regarding what he called "the cultural logic of late capitalism." The link between politics and urban form that Sorkin thought could and should be repaired, Jameson saw had been replaced by a spatial condition that was "something like a mutation in built space itself."[9] One bore witness to—indeed, one experienced—one's own inability to inhabit and move through a legible urban space. Jameson thought that the tension in this condition had an explanatory power. Sorkin and his contributors just wanted their old promenades back.[10]

These positions give two different interpretations of how late-modern architecture related to the construction of disciplinary and cultural meaning in the early 1990s. On the one hand, the loss of an ability to participate in and enact the city's legibility was seen as an architectural failure. On the other hand, architecture demonstrated a broader explanatory power in this failure. In both instances, a crisis of meaning was seen to be precipitated by the atrium: the appearance of the private in place of—and on the scale of—public space, an indifference to the outside this condition brought with it, and a sense of entrapment and bewilderment experienced by the loss of conventional limits or boundaries.

While these interpretations have themselves gained the status of cultural artifacts, there is a different and perhaps more brutally straightforward account of what the atrium's appearance has meant for architecture and for culture. Rather than seeing it as responsible for a breakdown in meaning and legibility, or being negatively symbolic of it, the atrium can be framed as it was for the presidential candidate: as a business proposition. The Trump Tower development took advantage of an approach to urban planning that emerged in New York City in the early 1960s, offering an exchange between an increase in the allowable floor area of developments and the provision of publicly accessible spaces, atriums among them, that would remain privately owned and maintained. While legally the atrium of Trump Tower must remain open to the public during designated hours, it can be closed for private events up to four times a year.[11] What was perhaps most confronting about the candidate closing the atrium for his campaign launch was that the economic power of real estate development was bluntly parlayed into the political power of brand and personality.

While this action may seem exceptional, its possibility was always embedded within the commercial and regulatory structure that produced the tower. As such, it effectively forecloses certain debates regarding the political merits of various forms of postmodern architecture that had fixated the discipline during the 1980s. In her account of architecture and politics in the Reagan era, Mary McLeod characterized these debates as being focused on an assumption that architectural form could be considered "either a critical or affirmative tool independent of social and economic processes."[12]

To be sure, by the mid-1980s, urban studies had begun to tackle the economic processes of urban redevelopment and the kind of politics they represented. One of Sorkin's contributors, Mike Davis, criticized what he saw as Jameson's fetishization of the formal qualities of Portman's atrium hotels, rather than accounting for the ways in which they were products of speculative investments that significantly changed the relationship between architecture and its urban role.[13] Yet, in the debate that ensued, and others like it, architecture—as profession, as process, and as formal and material object—drifted further away as a focus of critical concern, buildings being seen as largely symbolic of processes and structures whose logic lay elsewhere.[14] Kenny Cupers, Catharina Gabrielsson, and Helena Mattsson have articulated the problem this approach presents, one which arises from "a common misunderstanding that architecture (unlike the city) is a phenomenon set apart from policy, regulations, and processes of governance."[15] Other critics and historians have also outlined positions which provide more nuanced ways of understanding architecture's relationship to the social, political, organizational, and economic structures of postmodernism and neoliberalism. For example, Sylvia Lavin has analyzed the ways in which the bureaucratic conditions of postmodernization produced the postmodernist idea of "architecture itself,"[16] and Reinhold Martin has reconsidered what he calls the discursive formation of postmodernism through architecture's "refractory prism."[17]

The concerns of this book intersect with these positions. Portman's atriums and the importance of Jameson's critique of postmodernism are the most obvious overlaps, but this book's framing of the atrium's importance goes further than the invocation of what have now become iconic architecture and iconic discourse.[18] In its concept, form, and materials, and in the ways it was procured and designed in the offices of many architects, the atrium accompanied large-scale shifts in the way architecture would be practiced and what it would produce through the 1970s and '80s, the most intense period of change in "policy, regulations, and processes of governance." These included shifts in the understanding of architectural form and its technical parameters, with new knowledge and forms of expertise developing through the way in which the atrium was codified and regulated, and how its technical performance was understood and measured. Regulations governing the practice of architecture also changed, as it was opened to new forms of competition and business opportunity. And the atrium enabled the development of organizational strategies that drew from the realization that its material qualities had increasingly significant bearing on the comportment of inhabitants and users to the kinds of life they would lead and the kinds of work they would perform, together with the professional and social relationships these entailed.

The atrium gives these issues a historically situated material and spatial figure, and a particular method of investigating them. It is not simply a large indoor space as might be required by a specific function or type, such as the foyer in a theater, the concourse in a transit station, or the vault of a glasshouse, arcade, or shopping mall. Unlike these kinds of spaces, the atrium does not necessarily belong functionally to the building types in which it appears. An office building or a hotel can contain an atrium or not and still function as office building or hotel. Rather, in the way it articulates a relationship between inside and outside, an atrium makes possible specific activities, forms of work, forms of inhabitation, and ways of being. These are framed in each material and symbolic instance as simultaneously an act of opening and an act of enclosure. An atrium hotel can offer a range of activities and a kinetic visual experience that indicate to a hotel patron that they need not venture into the city outside to have an "urban" experience. An atrium in an office building can offer enticements for employees to interact away from their desks, emphasizing informal communications and social interaction as part of the fabric of work. These conditions are not neutral or given. Rather, they arise from methods of articulating, organizing, and deploying architecture to achieve specific ends which may change. A publicly accessible space—at least by the letter of a zoning regulation—can also become, quite literally, a political platform.

Rather than being a type of space with fixed characteristics, the atrium operates as what Bernhard Siegert has defined as a cultural technique. Referring to conventions of architectural enclosure, Siegert writes, "There is no such thing as *the* house, or the house as such; there are only historically and culturally contingent cultural techniques of shielding oneself and processing the distinction between inside and outside."[19] In his seminal book on the atrium from 1983, Richard Saxon called it "one of the generic building forms of the late twentieth century."[20] In its historically and culturally contingent manifestation, the atrium provided new material and symbolic techniques for processing the distinction between inside and outside. This processing also operated in relation to architecture's disciplinarity. Saxon recognized that the atrium's importance in contemporary architecture had as much to do with new forms of architectural knowledge and expertise as it did with the possibilities of new building forms.

★★★

The chapters of the book are organized around a series of gerunds to capture the active processing the atrium occasions, the idea that it is a mediator of people, things, and discourses. The book begins with "Forming," an account of how, in the late 1960s, the qualities and potentials of architectural form began to be defined via methods of computation. Researchers assessed the potentials of what they called the court form, a perimeter of built volume with a void in the middle, arguing that it provided more efficient use of land and better urban amenity at higher density when compared with the modernist stalwarts of tower and slab. As such the court form underpinned an approach to urban design and development that would increasingly use mathematical and scientific framings to equate built form with different kinds of performance. At the same time, critiques of the positivism of this kind of approach found in the court form a type that could be seen to have irreducibly architectural characteristics. The court appeared as ground against the figure of dense built fabric, a characteristic pattern of cities before modernism, and one that contained a spatial potential that could be revalued. In this tension between positivism and critical reflection, between the externally imposed parameters of numerical processing and the internal, architectural ones of disciplinary technique, the court form prefigured the problematic of the atrium building in the late twentieth century.

The three chapters that follow trace different aspects of this tension between the performative demands placed on buildings and the ways in which the practice of architecture negotiated the shifts that these occasioned. Chapter 2, "Regulating," explores the way in which atriums were seen to violate many of the conventions and codes that governed safety in the event of fire: as a large-scale, undivided space, the atrium risked the rapid spread of fire and smoke through a building. In the late 1970s, architects, engineers, and fire safety professionals in the United States and the United Kingdom responded to the increasing prevalence of atrium buildings by working to define a new approach to fire regulation. The safety problems of the atrium offered an incitement to these professionals to develop new techniques and technologies which increasingly involved a shift away from the application of established rules of safety toward an approach based in the validation of a building's safety performance. This shift meant that engineers and regulators developed new claims to expertise at a time when regulation was being opened to competition. Architects also found themselves operating in a different commercial environment and on a different risk footing, as the consequences of their design decisions were not necessarily backed by a definitive regulatory apparatus.

Chapter 3, "Conditioning," considers the environmental performance of the atrium building. Through the 1970s, when the energy consumption of buildings became a critical issue, the atrium became the focus of energy reduction strategies. In being an ambiguous, indoor/outdoor space, an atrium could help lower energy costs through achieving thermal balance by passive means. It also opened the way for different design approaches to illumination and ventilation, especially in office buildings which had been conventionally designed as sealed and air-conditioned. With the emergence of sick building syndrome, the sealed building was increasingly equated with poor health outcomes for occupants. The atrium offered the opportunity for building occupants to be more engaged in adjusting their immediate environment themselves, and, as such, in challenging assumptions regarding what constituted a comfortable workplace. Guided by research, architects were able to demonstrate their professional expertise by deploying the atrium as a design technique in a context where the indoor environment was becoming a complex social, political, and technical issue.

The engagement of building occupants with their environment was not simply a question of their empowerment, however. Chapter 4, "Organizing," explores how the planning of office space progressively involved the entrainment of employees into the various ideologies of business and management used by organizations. The atrium's ambiguity and indeterminacy—positive qualities from an energy and environmental standpoint—increasingly underpinned the different forms of flexibility that organizations demanded. Atriums offered the ability to refurbish and upgrade office buildings to respond to new technological demands, and to experiment with different configurations of work environments amid programs of corporate change. Often on a vast scale, atriums enclosed employees in a context of work whose boundaries were becoming less distinct from the world outside, these all-encompassing spaces emphasizing social interaction as the currency of the knowledge worker.

While chapters 2, 3, and 4 consider the ways in which calculation, measurement, and performance came to the fore through the 1970s and '80s, chapter 5, "Cultivating," reflects on the consequences of these shifts for architecture as a discipline. It considers how the atrium allowed "nature" to infiltrate buildings as an artificial, staged condition. Whatever its manifestations, from mature greenhouse to potted plant arrangement to ersatz garden, these versions of nature mediated the relationship between occupants and their mode of occupation, becoming increasingly more prominent than architecture's own means of signifying this relationship.

Each chapter begins with specifics: an incident, object, or pronouncement that sets up the shape of the discussion to follow. Sometimes this means an extended focus on debates amongst professionals, and at other times the material conditions of buildings are given more attention. Across the chapters, the selection of examples and case studies has been driven by their prominence within the different strands of discourse that are the focus of each chapter. Alongside canonical examples, atrium buildings that are less well known are also given attention because they articulate a theme or problem in a useful way. Because of the increasing ubiquity of atrium buildings through the 1970s and '80s, comprehensiveness or breadth has not been an aim,[21] and the book intentionally focuses on the issues the atrium presented in commercial buildings in the Northern Hemisphere.[22] These methodological approaches are supported throughout by scholarship that takes as its interest the technical and the bureaucratic as the basis for a renewed understanding of historical change in architecture, and that is attentive to a situated account of the relationship between architecture and sociopolitics.

A particular approach has been taken to the use of images. Diagrams have been included where they are useful to illustrate important technical concepts. Where available, photographs have been sourced that show buildings near the time of their completion and that emphasize a range of different approaches to depicting the atrium as an architectural space. In some instances new drawings have been included to emphasize the spatial and structural qualities of particular atriums.

As the void that emerged within a range of building types in the late twentieth century, the atrium draws attention to certain mechanisms that have had profound but often unacknowledged impacts on and through buildings: mechanisms of calculation and risk, of regulation, of expertise and professionalism, of business and commerce, and of research and knowledge.[23] These mechanisms have been actively formed, debated, and enacted in architecture. Akin to the atrium itself, architecture is seen as a discipline that operates in the distinction between what belongs within it and what is deemed to be outside of it, a distinction that has been actively and continually processed.

1

Forming

To consider the *emergence* of the atrium building, we shall not construct a historical lineage that stretches back across time, no matter how attractive it is to connect the atrium to its roots in the Roman *domus*, or to the arcades and greenhouses of the nineteenth century that inspired the design of many atrium buildings.[1] We shall be concerned with late twentieth-century problems, such as the one posed by Leslie Martin, professor and head of the architecture department at Cambridge University, and Lionel March, an architect and mathematician. In 1966 they asked: "What built forms make the best use of land?"[2] The question was posed in relation to a series of research projects that looked at different scales of architectural and urban organization, and the answer was surprising.[3] It was not the modernist icons of tall tower or slab block. Rather, the built form that made the best use of land was what they called the court form, a perimeter of built volume with a void in the middle. By modeling architectural forms within the parameters given by building controls, including setbacks, access to light, and floor area ratios,[4] they showed that high urban density could be achieved with buildings of much lower height than was thought to be possible, and the arrangement of the court form, they argued, would provide better urban amenity with distinct, objective, and demonstrable advantages over towers and slabs.

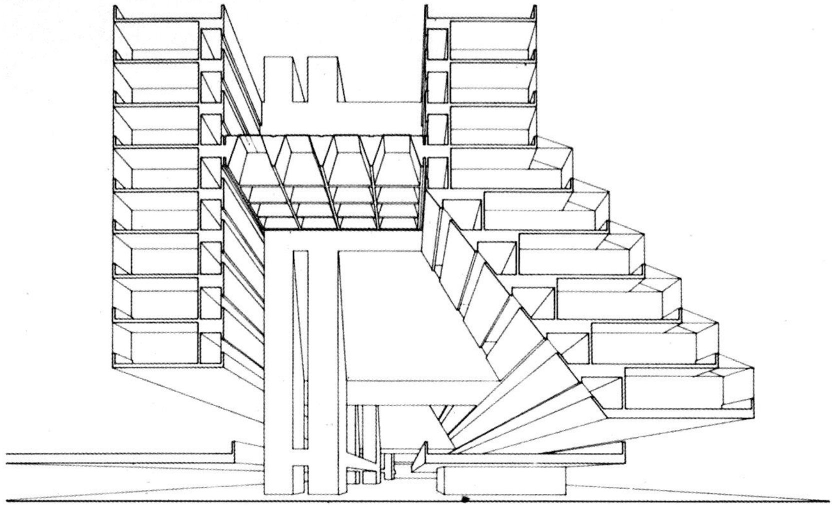

Figure 1.1 Design for National and Government Centre, Whitehall, London. Leslie Martin, 1965. Source: Leslie Martin, *Whitehall: A Plan for the National and Government Centre* (London: Her Majesty's Stationery Office, 1965), 55. UK Open Government Licence v3.0.

Martin had shown these advantages in one of his most audacious designs. In 1965 he drew up schematic plans to construct a new government center at Whitehall in London, proposing a linked array of low, court-form buildings.[5] The design's radicality was manifest less in the proposal to demolish the existing Whitehall buildings and consolidate a vast area of central London into a megastructure-like assembly than in the way such a move was justified. In the words of Dean Hawkes, a member of the Cambridge research team: "The act of adding [individual sites] together allows a <u>maximum permissible envelope</u> with greater <u>Built Volume Factor</u> to be generated than would otherwise be possible."[6] Hawkes's language was striking. The idea of a "built volume factor"—a numerical expression of the relationship between built form, volume, and land area—indicated an entirely new approach to how the efficiency and value of different built forms could be understood and articulated. No longer were there to be assumptions based in precedent or experience, or faith in "manifestos of the second machine age" as the Cambridge researchers put it.[7] Rather, through mathematical modeling and calculation, the team would seek to find an objective and rational basis for evaluating the effectiveness and applicability of a range of architectural and urban forms. Their research was formalized with the establishment of Cambridge University's Centre for Land Use and Built Form Studies (LUBFS), which Martin and March founded in 1967.[8] Into the 1970s, the team would develop increasingly sophisticated computer models that incorporated a range of different parameters, from energy and environmental performance and building use patterns to urban circulation and zoning, producing models that could govern design and planning across the scales of building, city, and region. The LUBFS team declared that "our knowledge can be more certain, our predictions more reasonable, our assumptions more explicit, and our understanding more aware of its shortcomings."[9]

These mathematical modeling and computational techniques shifted questions of architectural form into a new register, away from order and composition, away, even, from the more programmatic modernist versions of function and efficiency, and toward a new calculus of architecture and its performance.

While these studies were being developed, the court form also became prominent in other discourses that challenged such positivism. Its specific spatial characteristics, the inside-outside qualities of the court itself, were seen to be particular and irreducibly architectural, inscribing, for instance, qualities of solid and void that could be drawn in figure-ground. This analytical technique became particularly prevalent in studies that sought to challenge the tenets of modernist urbanism by returning to more traditional understandings of urban form.

At this time the court form pointed in two seemingly contradictory directions. On the one hand it offered a way to move beyond what LUBFS researchers considered to be misleading design approaches by allowing for a more logical and rigorous analysis of design problems. On the other hand, it pointed to techniques of architectural design that had been suppressed or forgotten in modernism's supposedly rationalist approach. The court form thus held within it the tension inherent in architectural design "after" modernism. It offered a way to formalize a range of parameters that sat external to architecture but nonetheless increasingly governed how buildings were materialized—numerical parameters of regulation, codification, and technical performance. It also offered a particular spatial arrangement that had a typological lineage within architecture. The court form pointed to a historical reserve of related formal arrangements that could be adapted via the techniques of architectural design.

In this way the court form sets up the problematics of the atrium building. In roofing over the court void and materializing a reinvented architectural space, the atrium building increasingly became subject to the frames of regulation and performance that were part of computational methods. In many ways it became the architectural culmination of the potentials the Cambridge researchers saw in the court form. By dint of the enclosure of the void, in every instance the atrium building also became an architectural design proposition, at once a novel arrangement and one bound by technique to disciplinary expectations.

★★★

As part of efforts to understand how built form related to land use, Martin and March's colleague Dean Hawkes posed a fundamental question: what is the relationship between built form and the way in which it can be controlled? While some form of legislated building control had been in operation in cities including London and New York since the middle of the nineteenth century, their purpose was to set the maximum allowable built envelope on any given site in order to preserve basic urban amenity. For example, the aim of New York's 1916 Zoning Ordinance was to preserve daylight access to streets by specifying frontage heights and setbacks. London regulations had set a cap on the maximum allowable height of buildings, and increasingly sought to encode values such as access to daylight, ventilation, and noise control.[10]

A significant shift occurred around the middle of the twentieth century when ratios began to be introduced into building control. The floor space index and daylight factor were introduced in the 1947 Holden-Holford Plan for the Reconstruction of the City of London, and the floor area ratio would appear in planning legislation in New York in 1961.[11] These ratios controlled the amount of floor area that could be developed on an individual site and allowed more sophisticated control of total building bulk and layout, though basic volumetric rules governing frontage, setback, or height would largely remain. Nevertheless, these new indices opened the way for a range of complying building forms and arrangements to be developed and analyzed, whereas previous codes had effectively defined envelopes, and therefore building forms, via prescribed geometries or historically embedded approaches to urban form.[12]

The introduction of the floor area ratio enabled a new idea in building control: the ability to trade area for other urban amenities. The 1961 New York code allowed floor area bonuses to be given in exchange for publicly accessible space within individual sites. Hawkes referred to this as a "subtle legal bribery," noting that it provided "a means of 'encouraging' speculators to assist in creating the planners' vision."[13] Nevertheless, Hawkes concluded, the real issue was that "the general effect of the kind of building bulk legislation we have at the present time is to channel the forms of development into a restricted range of choice."[14] He argued that this restriction stemmed from the graphical means of representation that made the underlying codes visible and understandable in architectural terms, and these means tended to present the volumetric translation of the codes as the acceptable architectural envelope. Instead, seizing on the idea that a parameter like floor area ratio was not a preconceived form, Hawkes proposed: "The capacities and conveniences of a mathematical model, manipulated by computer, might be more effective in indicating to the practitioner the whole range of options available to him in the solution of a particular program, on a specific site, within the context of the currently accepted social values and standards."[15]

A mathematical model would not be subject to the kinds of formal preconceptions that were seen in graphical representations. Such a model could produce a whole range of possible built forms that would comply with given codes and could absorb adjustments and new parameters as codes changed or other control mechanisms were introduced. Hawkes went further: "In this event the existence of a control system, in the same 'language' as the design model, would be, to say the least, useful."[16]

This somewhat understated conclusion encapsulates the nature of the shift being proposed by the LUBFS team: if the control function of a mechanism such as a building code could be understood as the combination of different parameters, then built forms themselves could emerge from their manipulation. The underpinning language of form was the mathematical model that could compute a potentially limitless number of inputs and output a range of forms based on these.

Extending what was, literally, formative work, Martin and March assumed that plot ratio, the British equivalent to floor area ratio, was an index for the best or most effective use of land. To test this, they experimented with arrays of what they considered to be three fundamental types of built form: the pavilion (or tower), the street (or row), and the court (or perimeter building). Each had specific conditions with respect to its form: "The pavilion is finite in its plan form; the street extends, potentially, infinitely along one axis; the court infinitely along two."[17] They arrayed these built forms over a fixed site and spaced them consistently according to an acceptable angle of daylight penetration.

Four-story towers arrayed in this way gave a plot ratio of 2:1, that is, twice as much floor area as site area. The array of court buildings of the same height yielded a plot ratio of 3:1, three times as much floor area as site area. The key to this higher ratio was the court form's extensibility in two directions. By contrast, the pavilion form remained bounded, extra height or a deeper plan being the only means to increase floor area. As such, Martin and March concluded: "Assuming for a moment that both forms of building lend themselves equally to internal planning, it becomes clear that the building form can have a pronounced effect on the total floor space possible on any given site."[18] With this simple experiment, and its startling conclusion, they inverted an assumption that had accompanied the pavilion's extruded form, the modernist tower: through increased height, this form would be the key to increased density, and therefore growth, in urban areas. The inversion was literal; it was the void, or court, at the center of the perimeter building that was the key to "better," or more effective, land use. The court offered access to daylight while, morphologically, allowing the built form's extensibility in two directions. A key discovery was that the same plot ratios of pavilion forms could be achieved at lower heights with court forms. Further, through mathematical modeling, they showed that increasing the height of pavilions, that is, creating towers in the hope of

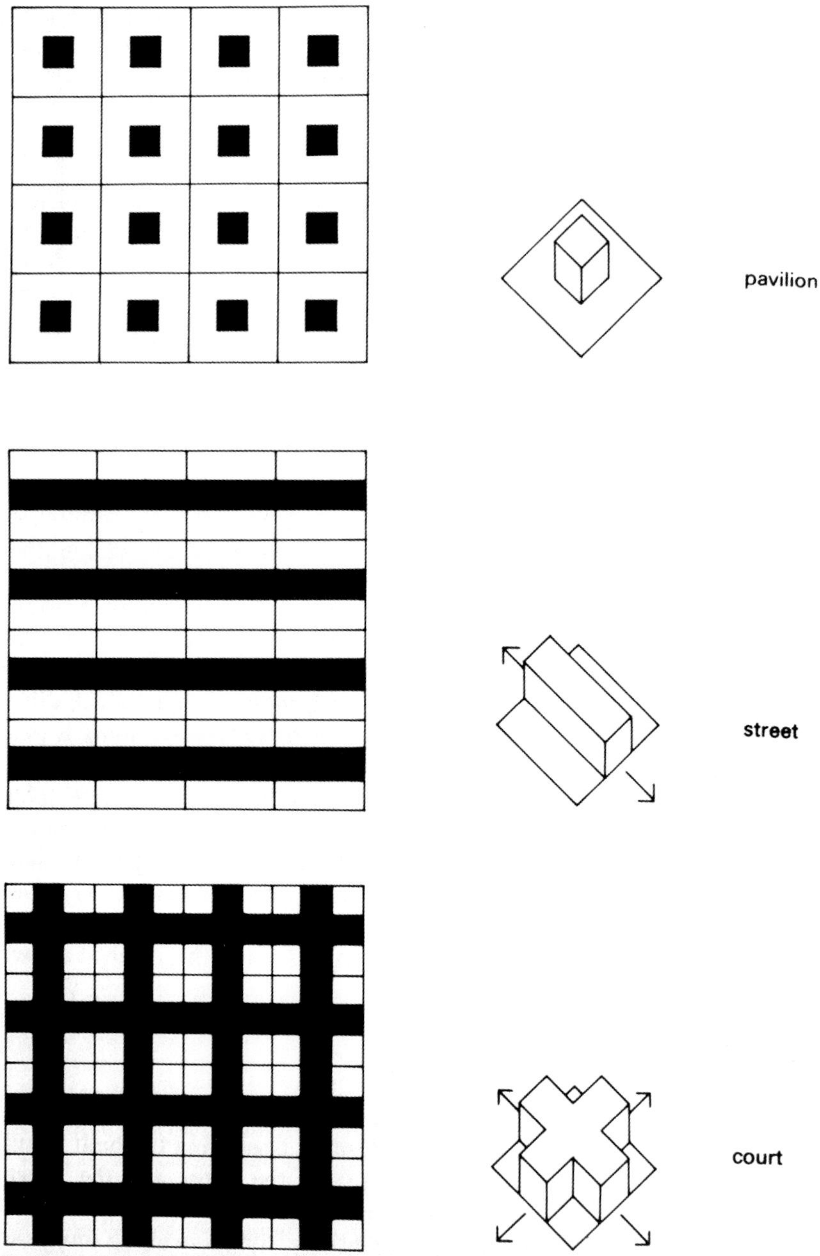

Figure 1.2 Built form studies: pavilion, street, and court. Drawings by Lionel March. Source: Leslie Martin and Lionel March, eds., *Urban Space and Structures* (Cambridge: Cambridge University Press, 1972), 36. Reproduced with permission of Cambridge University Press through PLSclear.

more efficient land use, was a law of diminishing returns.[19] When considered in terms of the same built potential, that is, the ratio of the floor area of the built form to the site area, they were also able to show that pavilion or tower forms exhibited much deeper plans than the street or court forms. From this they concluded: "Many of the so-called advantages of deep plan in tower blocks may thus be afterthoughts rather than fundamental generators of the building form, for the deep plan is the inevitable outcome of using the pavilion form."[20] And as March would later explain, the research "established the notion that high-rise building was not the outcome of land shortage, but of particular relationships between site and building volume."[21] In their argument, towers and deep-plan pavilions were the result of a misconception regarding density, their form and its characteristics the unsatisfactory outcome of a relationship between built volume and site that was poorly understood.

Martin and March developed these initial findings with what they called non-prismatic forms. These were defined in terms of a pyramid, a truncated pyramid (with a flattened top), and what they termed a generalized pavilion, which was a truncated pyramid with an orthogonal tower form extruded from its top. With these more architectural forms, Martin and March made a further move which advanced their case for the efficiency of the court form. Each non-prismatic form was given a complementary anti-form, essentially an inversion of the formal figure in a void condition. They showed that an array of generalized pavilion forms would be matched in built volume by an array of modified anti-forms of much lower height. Indeed, the extruded tower element of the pavilion forms could be done away with completely by the capacity of the anti-form voids. This occurred through a neat formal trick. The pyramidal angle exerted a negative effect on the overall volumetric capacity of the form. If we imagine a podium at the base of a tower, its pyramidal form comes about via a subtraction of potential built form, the angles a result of the attempt to maintain daylight penetration to a street. As anti- or inverted form, however, the pyramidal angle adds built volume to the courtyard

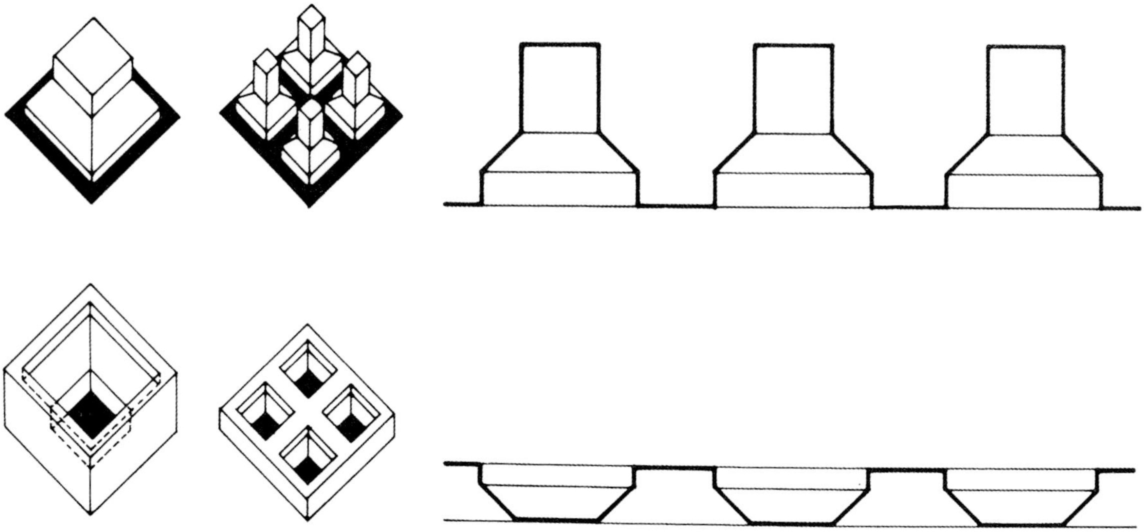

Figure 1.3 Built form studies: non-prismatic forms. Drawings by Lionel March. Source: Leslie Martin and Lionel March, eds., *Urban Space and Structures* (Cambridge: Cambridge University Press, 1972), 20. Reproduced with permission of Cambridge University Press through PLSclear.

void without inhibiting access to daylight. As Martin and March somewhat blithely put it: "Thus it may be seen, in this example, that the generalised pyramid solution would need to be nearly three times the height of its anti-form if the same amount of built volume were to be provided on any given site."[22]

The research moved beyond the assumptions that lay behind the analysis of the initial, orthogonal built forms—that the possibilities for internal planning could be assumed to be the same for each—as the inverted pyramid gave the court form greater floorplate flexibility within the described constraints. The variation in section given by the inverted pyramid translated into the availability of overall variance in layout possibilities. What was given as a simple mathematical illustration—the relationship between form and anti-form—could be seen to have profound architectural implications.

It is important to emphasize, as the authors did, that these studies were abstract and theoretical. As March wrote: "Buildings are complex artefacts. Most are unique. Generalisations about buildings are not easy to make. It may help to look instead at *built forms* which are not buildings. Built forms are mathematical or quasi-mathematical models . . . which are used to represent buildings to any required degree of complexity in theoretical studies."[23] Such mathematical models had an application, but to a degree that was limited by their nature as models.[24] As March would claim, "in practice they may help clear away some of the misleading 'rules of thumb' which frequently lurk behind design decisions, and they may help to replace these by more cautious generalisations, but, be warned—these may be equally misleading if results and conclusions are extrapolated beyond the simplifying assumptions of the original model."[25]

In the Cambridge team's terms, the potential of this approach to the analysis of form was clear: built forms derived with these methods offered a range of choice to architects, and these forms could then be used as the basis of design decisions. But it was precisely the nexus between mathematical modeling and decisions an architect might make, indeed, the creative act of architecture itself, that dogged the Cambridge team from the beginning. At the time, conservative critics leapt to defend the very "rules of thumb" that March saw could be overcome with judicious, mathematically based analyses. Seizing on March's nod to Russian constructivism in the foreword to a volume of collected papers of the LUBFS team,[26] Roger Scruton labeled what he saw as reductive, technocratic prescriptions "Stalinist,"[27] and David Watkin described Martin's Whitehall plan as a "gigantic rationalistically constructed beehive."[28]

More recent critiques have situated the work of LUBFS within the history of computation in architecture. Sean Keller has linked the work of March in particular to avant-garde formal and aesthetic experimentation, increasingly computer-based, that took hold from the 1980s.[29] The result of LUBFS research more generally—and that of other university-based research centers that pioneered architectural computing—has been both more banal and more pervasive. It has underpinned the development of computer-aided design, modeling, and analysis programs that, LUBFS member Philip Steadman has noted, now comprise the toolkit of architects.[30] All buildings designed with CAD systems—straight or bendy, orthogonal or canted, avant-garde or commercial—are underpinned by the algorithmic encoding of form. And further, the systems thinking that led to these outcomes has had much to do with the embedding of concepts of calculation, regulation, and risk in everyday architectural practice.[31]

★★★

Beyond the rationalized value and utility of the court form, it is worth reflecting further on what the form does formally, so to speak. In the simplest terms, the court form establishes a relationship between a perimeter of built volume and a void enclosed by it. This sets up an outside-inside-outside relationship. There is an outside to the form, defined by its exterior boundary, which is proper to the urban. There is also an outside condition—the void—held within the form itself, which is qualitatively different from the outside of the form. Even in these simple terms the court form contains a spatial potential that is not exhausted by its mathematical description or a code-based regulatory apparatus. What was seen to be optimal from a regulatory perspective—the form that made the best use of land—produced within itself something in excess of that determination, something whose qualitative, spatial dimensions could be exploited architecturally and urbanistically.

The aim in describing the court form in this way is to establish its architectural specificity, one that some thought had been obliterated in the turn toward a certain kind of mathematical decision making. Or, as the critic Alan Colquhoun wrote in 1972: "Architectural theory has been dominated for the last decade or so by various forms of determinism or populism, neither of which recognizes architecture as constituting a cultural entity in its own right."[32] In an earlier article from 1967 entitled "Typology and Design Method," Colquhoun grappled with how to specify what this "in its own right" of architecture would be, interrogating the concept of typology, which had become the focus of renewed attention in the discipline. Colquhoun framed the debate on form and method in architecture in much the same way as Martin and March had a year earlier by recognizing the contemporary desire to overcome what he called "intuitive methods of design" in response to the increasing complexity of problems architects were addressing. For Colquhoun, those intuitive methods were a leftover from a foundational contradiction within modernist orthodoxy, which, he argued, held together "biotechnical determinism on the one hand and free expression on the other." As he wrote, "What seems to have happened is that, in the act of giving a new validity to the demands of function as an extension of nature's mode of operation, a vacuum has been left where previously there was a body of traditional practice."[33]

The LUBFS team had clearly attempted to overcome this contradiction with what they considered to be better definitions of the complexity of problems,[34] but, as Colquhoun argued, there remained an issue with the idea that "the more rigorously the general physical or mathematical laws are applied to the solution of design problems the less it is necessary to have a mental picture of the final form." He recognized that such laws were themselves constructs and were only "valid so long as events do not prove them to be wrong."[35]

Colquhoun sought a way through this conundrum by making a distinction between general configurations of form that may be governed by mathematical relationships, and actual or detailed configurations,[36] the realm of an architect's decision making that was also the realm of how architecture could be represented as, and be representative of, a particular configuration in a "socially recognizable way"—involving the "mental picture of the final form"—as part of architecture's cultural remit. As he clarified, "It follows that the representational systems which are developed are, in a real sense, independent of the quantifiable facts of the environment."[37] The LUBFS team might well have agreed with him. Steadman has pointed out that the preoccupations of the team were wider than has been appreciated, that there was no restriction against being "an architectural scientist on a Monday and a painter on a Tuesday."[38]

As this remark shows, what LUBFS has been critiqued for—the collapsing of mathematical determinations of form onto those properly belonging to the representational or cultural—is most usefully understood as a critical distinction germane to the problem with which it was grappling: the mathematical and the representational were distinct domains of architectural knowledge and action. This held open the idea that architects may again be able to access a store of "traditional practice," or what Colquhoun characterized as a typological approach to design—"a knowledge of past solutions applied to related problems"[39]—whilst still working within relationships held together in an "optimal" way, such as those described mathematically by the court form.

The idea of the social and cultural recognizability or mental image of form has often been seen as a problematic and retrograde aspect of the renewed interest in typology that gained strength through the 1970s and

'80s, springing from the perceived continuity between architectural and urban form that Aldo Rossi, for example, sought to emphasize.[40] As Lawrence Barth has argued: "Typological description and classification found itself provisionally subordinated to the urban plan, registered through a particular set of visual materials that emphasized figure-ground studies and perspective drawings of iconic urban spaces."[41]

The court's formal distinctiveness relative to its modernist counterparts of pavilion (or tower) and street (or slab) resonated with this understanding of typology. When drawn in an urban configuration, the court form provided a strong figure-ground inscription with a clear delineation of solid and void. In their 1978 book *Collage City*, Colin Rowe and Fred Koetter would use such a method of delineation to critique the modernist urbanism of tower and slab.[42] Focusing on modernism's immediate postwar reappraisal of the idea of the "city core" and using Le Corbusier's 1945 plan for the French city of Saint-Dié as their example, they would highlight the necessity of the bounded void to ensure the articulation of urban space, critiquing modernism's formal inadequacy that was manifest in what they called the "the dilemma of the free standing building, the space occupier attempting to act as space definer . . . an acropolis of sorts which is attempting to perform as some version of an agora!"[43] To drive home their point, they juxtaposed the plan for Saint-Dié with the Italian city of Parma, arguing that "the two of them together might, sometimes, almost present themselves as the alternative reading of some Gestalt diagram illustrating the fluctuations of the figure-ground phenomenon."[44] And in another provocative juxtaposition, Le Corbusier's Unité d'Habitation in Marseille (1952) was pitted against Giorgio Vasari's Uffizi in Florence (1581), the latter being seen as the "jelly mold" of the former.[45]

Despite this critique, the debate about form in the context of a renewed interest in typology is not relevant because of the potential rediscovery of the value of solid and void as against the failures of the modernist freestanding object, as if the rationally premiated court form could be

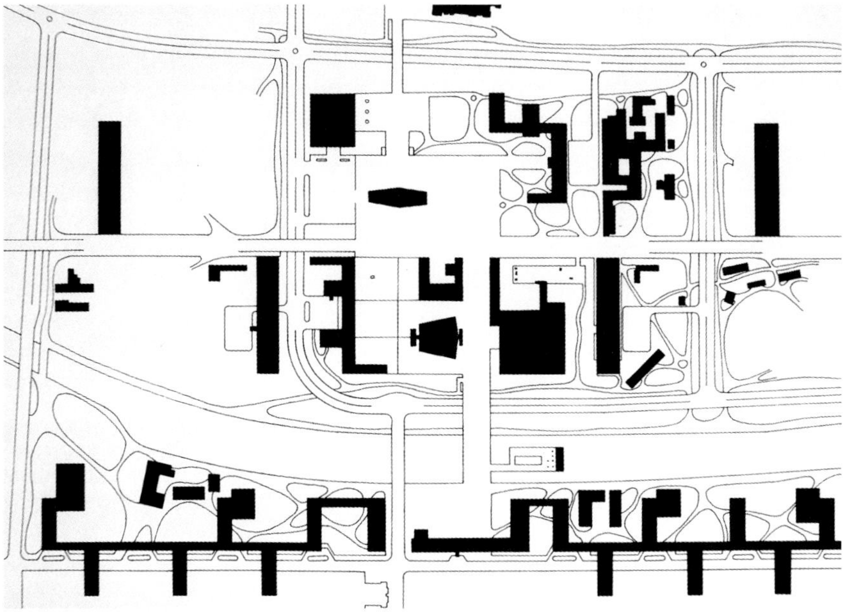

Figure 1.4 Figure-ground drawing of Le Corbusier's proposal for the town of Saint-Dié, France. Drawing by Wayne Copper, 1967. Source: *Cornell Journal of Architecture*, no. 2 (1982), plate. Courtesy Cornell University Department of Architecture.

Figure 1.5 Figure-ground drawing of Parma, Italy. Drawing by Wayne Copper, 1967. Source: *Cornell Journal of Architecture*, no. 2 (1982), plate. Courtesy Cornell University Department of Architecture.

accommodated simply by redrawing it as the historical form of continuity between architecture and the city. This is not what Colquhoun meant by a specific form relating to a store of traditional practice.

Rather, the aim in pursuing the court form through its relation to typology is to reapproach ways in which claims were made for its "efficiency." Aside from how it was mathematically justified or whether it was related to a larger program to rationalize architectural decision making, form can be seen to mediate a set of relationships between architecture's exterior and its interior. The court form organizes a set of external relationships and forces, specifically those of regulation and technical performance, and a spatial potential intrinsic to architecture, the specific inside-outside-inside characteristics that arise within the form.

This provides another way of understanding the gap between form as a general configuration and the specific decisions and actions that can flow from it. The relationship is not historical or formally continuous as Rossi might have it, nor even about the collagist accommodation of the new and the old, as per Rowe and Koetter. Rather, this relationship can be understood to be strategic. Colquhoun's "traditional practice" here becomes a specifically architectural mode of reasoning, what Barth has called "typological reasoning."[46] This mode governs how the architectural possibilities of form, organization, and materials might be related, through design, to the forces that impact architecture from the outside. Historically, it would recognize how particular architectural strategies exist within an organized field of decision making that itself had particular characteristics, such as the ones that obtained within LUBFS during the course of its research.

As we shall see in subsequent chapters, the strategic move of enclosing what might otherwise be an open void, or giving a space internal to a building the characteristics of an "outside," entailed complex and dynamic relationships between architectural materializations and broader socio-technical and political forces. That is, it entailed a particular way of processing distinctions, both spatially and in disciplinary terms, between inside and outside. This is one way of conceiving of how the atrium emerged, not simply from the court as abstract form, but from the culture of the discipline trying to absorb what increasingly sophisticated modes of calculation would mean for the mobilization of its "store of traditional practice." In encountering instances of architecture negotiating the relationship between calculation and materialization, we shall see that neither the supposed abstract certainty of calculation nor what could constitute a specifically architectural mode of reasoning go unchallenged or unchanged.

2

Regulating

In the early morning of 2 April 1973, a fire broke out in the Blue Max nightclub at John Portman's Hyatt Regency O'Hare hotel (1971) outside Chicago. A report on the blaze in the *Fire Journal* described the event in vivid detail:

> At approximately 4.30am, a maintenance employee discovered fire coming from the night club entrance into the atrium. He activated a manual fire alarm station, then pulled out a standpipe hose on the floor below and began playing water up the escalator opening towards the club entrance[.] . . . [V]isibility was down to approximately 10 feet in most areas of the atrium. Some guests had left their rooms and evacuated the building [via] stairways. Many guests were calling for help, and some had tied sheets together for escape over exterior balconies.[1]

The Hyatt Regency O'Hare fire marked the moment when fire engineers began focusing on the issues that the atrium, the quintessential space of 1970s hotel architecture across the globe, presented for life safety.[2] The vast space that had "exploded" the dreary hotel lobby[3] could quickly fill

Figure 2.1 Hyatt Regency O'Hare, Chicago. John Portman & Associates, 1971. © 1971 Alexandre Georges. Courtesy The Portman Archives.

with smoke, and fire could potentially spread through a building more quickly because the atrium connected spaces together. By 1984, fire code consultant Gregory Miller noted: "Within the last decade, the trend in architecture of providing atriums in buildings has probably spurred more discussion among those in the building code enforcement field concerning the philosophies, goals and methods of smoke control than any other topic."[4] Reactions revolved around the spatial novelty of the atrium. Engineering professor Paul DeCicco noted that "the way these spaces are set within major structures are extremely varied and limited only by the imagination of the designer,"[5] while others referred to "exotic architectural innovations"[6] and the problem that "we just do not seem to be able to stay abreast of all the new architectural innovations and designs."[7] DeCicco, who had written a report on the Hyatt Regency O'Hare nightclub fire and had evaluated the fire safety of Portman's design for the Times Square Marriott Marquis hotel in New York (1985),[8] remarked that "these new [atrium] designs come into direct conflict with almost all of the traditional principles governing life safety in building structures."[9]

What DeCicco had in mind was the way the scale and openness of the atrium went against separation and compartmentation as the core tenets of fire safety. Conventionally, for a building to be considered safe, its spaces should be subdivided or closed off from one another to aid fire and smoke containment, and to enable egress. The vast atriums engineers and code consultants were increasingly seeing provided continuous spaces rather than compartmentation. They gave architects the opportunity to combine a range of different functions and experiences, often giving them an urban feel. Two fire engineers who were researching smoke behavior in atriums put it in precise terms: "the latest trend in atrium design is the creation of a very large undivided volume within a structure, creating (visually and spatially) the ideal external environment—indoors."[10]

From a formal perspective, the atrium building was essentially a court with a roof over it. With this seemingly straightforward material change an abstract form had, suddenly, become very real, and decisions needed

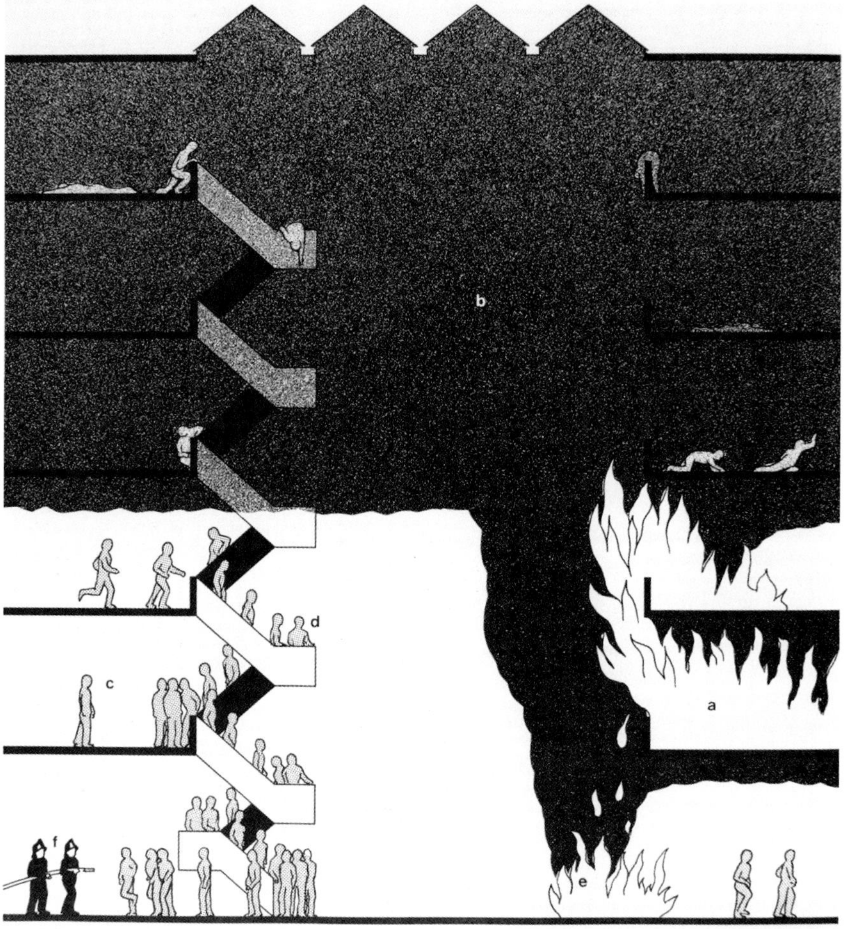

Figure 2.2 "Potential hazards in an ill conceived atrium." The drawing indicates problems of fire growth and spread (a, e), smoke build-up (b), safety of egress (c, d), and access and effectiveness in firefighting (f). Source: Richard Saxon, *Atrium Buildings: Development and Design* (London: Architectural Press, 1983), 92. Courtesy Richard Saxon.

to be made by architects, engineers, and building regulators to ensure its safety. Yet there was already a sense that these decisions would not be straightforward.

Building regulations such as fire safety codes are not simply the products of scientific development or the rational application of technical principles. Rather, as Liam Ross has argued, they are provisional agreements involving "concord and discord between a wide range of actors."[11] Regulations and codes are subject to interests that are often competing. As the atrium building became popular through the 1970s and '80s in the United States and the United Kingdom, discussions regarding its fire safety tracked a larger shift in the nature of regulation itself, which, as Ross has posited, changed "from an activity in which we recognise common threats, and develop universalised means to encounter them, to one through which we make calculated decisions balancing individual opportunities for profit and loss."[12]

The risks—and advantages—the atrium presented forced architects, engineers, and regulators to come to new kinds of agreements regarding how building codes would be formulated and applied. Through the 1980s, this was increasingly colored by the "opportunities" that competition and deregulation would unleash within the professions involved with buildings and their safety. The model of architecture and development Portman pioneered would become ratified in changes to architects' codes of conduct, and some architects would become more directly involved in market-oriented models of building development.

In this dynamic, the atrium became significant as a mediator of architectural spaces, building materials, safety technologies, regulatory codes, and professional practices. It would provide a context in which the conventional relationships between these components could be pulled apart and then reassembled, shifting the way architecture could be procured, designed, constructed, and deemed safe.

★★★

Figure 2.3 Marriott Marquis, New York, during celebrations to mark the building's opening. John Portman & Associates, 1985. © 1985 Unknown Photographer. Courtesy The Portman Archives.

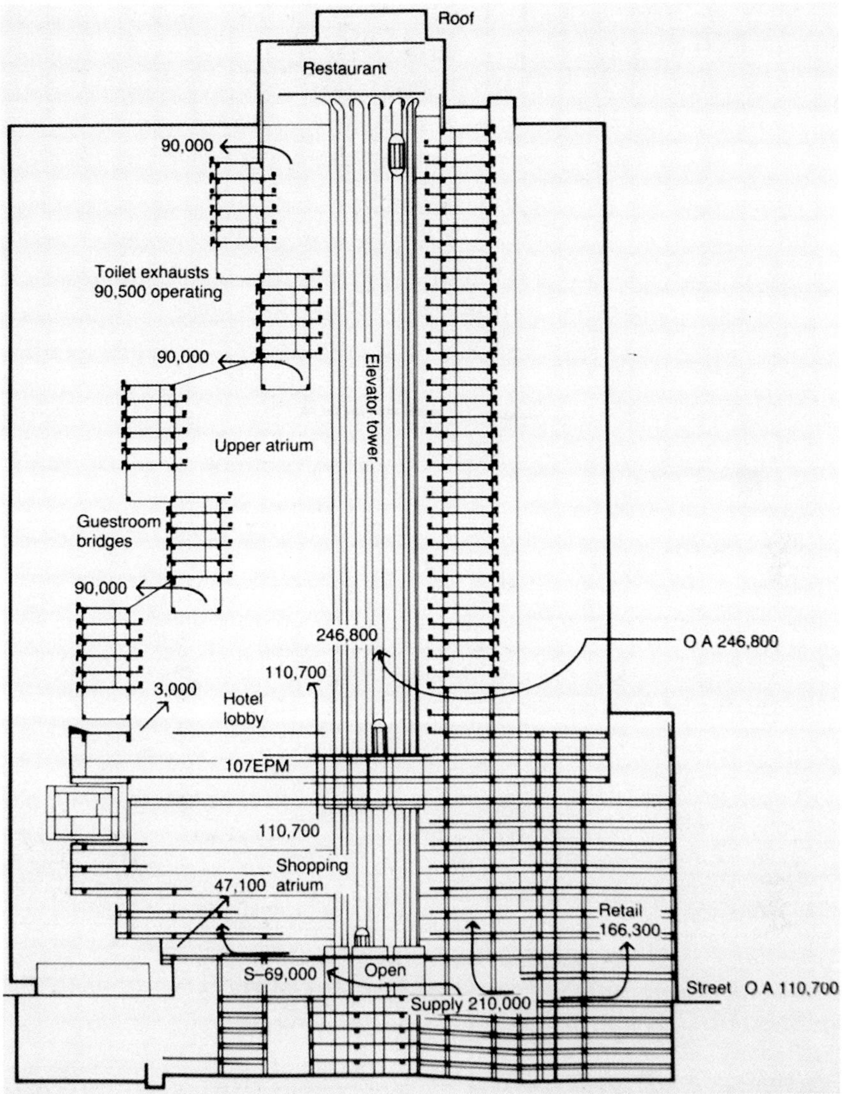

Figure 2.4 Diagram showing volumes of introduced and extracted air during fire, Marriott Marquis, New York. Analysis by Paul DeCicco and Robert J. Cressi. Source: Richard Saxon, *Atrium Buildings: Development and Design* (London: Architectural Press, 1983), 106. Courtesy Richard Saxon.

By the early 1980s, the four Model Building Codes used in the United States would recognize the atrium as a new spatial condition in a range of building types and outline requirements for compliance to enable egress, control smoke, and inhibit the spread of fire.[13] One of these, the Basic Building Code, was produced by the Building Officials and Code Administrators International (BOCA), an association of building code professionals that historically developed codes and supported their use by cities, states, and other government entities in the United States. To develop new code requirements for atriums, the BOCA established the Ad Hoc Committee on Atriums made up of BOCA members and other building industry professionals. Examining the committee's business and the commentary around the regulations they developed is instructive for understanding the problems the atrium presented for regulators, and the way in which these were articulated. As committee member and fire engineer John Degenkolb remarked, "A considerable amount of time was spent trying to develop a definition for the term 'atrium' with no success."[14] One thing the committee agreed on was that it was not a shopping mall, which, for code purposes, was limited to three levels. What confounded fire code professionals was that atriums came in many different shapes and sizes and appeared within a range of functions. Amidst this uncertainty, Degenkolb settled on his own, rather perfunctory definition: "An atrium would be a court with a lid on it."[15]

The invocation of the court form is significant because it brings a problem usually thought to be about a building's exterior within the building itself. Conventionally, a court is a void in the middle of a building open to the sky. In the event of a fire in the building surrounding it, a court of large volume was thought to enable smoke to dissipate to the open air. Existing codes stipulated minimum lateral dimensions of 40 feet to inhibit the spread of fire across a court, and there was no requirement for fire-protected openings onto it, though smaller courts would require such openings.[16]

Degenkolb noted how a member of the BOCA committee, someone he reported was a "prominent architect representing John Portman," wanted to leverage the existing code provision for open courts by arguing that interior spaces of 40 feet or more and up to six stories high should be designated "just part of the building,"[17] that is, not subject to any fire separation. This bold suggestion aligned the atrium with the morphology of the court but elided their material difference: the enclosing lid. Unless there was some sort of ventilation technology, the presence of the lid would not allow smoke to dissipate to the open air, thus presenting a potential safety risk.

As "landlord of downtown Atlanta"[18] and the original architect-developer, Portman had designed and built the first atrium hotel there in 1967, the Hyatt Regency.[19] A classic court form, the building featured four slabs of hotel rooms arranged around a roofed atrium that extended to the building's full, 22-story height. Gondola-like elevator cabs rose through the atrium in exposed shafts, providing a visual and kinetic spectacle. Sitting atop extensive convention facilities, the atrium contained an urban world in miniature: bars, restaurants, mature trees, cascading foliage, and even an aviary gave hotel patrons all they needed in air-conditioned comfort, effectively keeping them inside in a city beset by the social and racial fracturing of urban renewal.[20] Over subsequent years Portman would develop two further atrium hotels as well as commercial, wholesale, retail, office, and entertainment spaces in a development known as Peachtree Center, which would eventually extend over more than a dozen city blocks, its component parts connected by above-grade walkways.

While at the time there was no explicit fire code provision for a structure like the Hyatt Regency Atlanta, the audacious design was approved by the local fire department, and Portman would continue to use this precedent as he built further atrium hotels as part of extensive mixed-use urban developments across the United States through the 1970s. When safety codes were beginning to recognize the atrium at the end of that decade, the nature of Portman's influence was not lost on the fire safety profession. British fire surveyors E. Gordon Butcher and Alan C. Parnell remarked that Portman's firm had "met a wide range of '*opposition*' over the years from the various State and city enforcement officers which has built up to

Figure 2.5 Hyatt Regency, Atlanta. John Portman & Associates, 1967. © 1968 Alexandre Georges. Courtesy The Portman Archives.

quite a substantial package of '*answers*,' which has enabled them to continue with this building form."[21] Portman's answers were based on the idea that the openness and connectivity of the atrium would increase the visibility of a fire, which was then less likely to go undetected and could be attended to more easily. Egress could occur more quickly because more occupants were likely to see smoke or flames, and the volume of air in a large atrium could allow flames to cool and smoke to dissipate more effectively.[22] However, Parnell thought that the spectacle of Portman's atriums, in particular the prominence of gondola elevators, suppressed the existence of fire escape stairs, and he worried that the route to these stairs was via galleries open to the void space, increasing the exposure to smoke and flames.[23]

Regardless of this kind of disagreement, the influence of Portman's buildings and his mode of development was a sign that a shift was underway from compliance with absolute rules toward a negotiated agreement regarding the safety of building designs. Yet the BOCA committee still had to come to some determination regarding how the atrium should be treated in the code. They were attempting this not simply to codify an increasingly popular design, but to maintain the relevance and operability of the code in a broader sense. In doing so they considered technical factors based on empirical understanding and direct experience (including atrium fires such as the one at Portman's Hyatt Regency O'Hare), basic but often limited scientific testing, rules of thumb—architect William Tabler informed the committee that he had been designing atriums with three stories open to the atrium void, so that was adopted into the code[24]—and an allowance for exceptions. The rules for fire safety in atriums were eventually codified as a synthesis of all of these factors: functions within the atrium needed low fire hazard designation, smoke exhaustion (with standby power) was required along with smoke detectors and monitored sprinkler systems, the distance to enclosed escape stairways was limited, interior material finishes were restricted, and only three stories could directly open to an atrium, with other levels needing to be sealed off.[25] In his summary of the changes that were incorporated into the code by 1981, DeCicco suggested that they "specify measures which do not make the design of atrium buildings safer than non-atrium buildings, instead they are directed to overcoming rather significant violations of what fire protection engineers have long held as the basics of fire safety."[26] And further, Miller pointed out that because of the way in which new code provisions were developed amongst architects, regulators, and fire experts, "the Codes are at least two years behind current technology."[27]

What emerges with the inclusion of atriums in the BOCA code is an engineering approach to fire safety. Having challenged the conventions of fire safety, the risks the atrium presented had to be mitigated by mechanical systems such as powered smoke exhaustion, sprinklers, and other means such as pressurized escape stairs. Yet these were not technical solutions so much as discursive propositions regarding safety. At that point, there was no conclusive technical proof that, when combined, these measures would mitigate the spread of smoke and fire in an atrium building, only an agreed proposition that they were necessary. And that agreement remained tenuous.

In their appraisal of the new codes, Butcher and Parnell, who in 1979 had published a key reference book on fire safety, noted that "the information on which fire protection measures are decided is fragmented and ill-digested."[28] Regarding the requirement that no more than three stories should be open to an atrium space, they suggested that this "rule"—which, as we have seen, was codified from a rule of thumb—could potentially cause fires to spread more easily. Radiant heat could travel between floors sealed off from the atrium, and the lack of air flow from floors closed to the atrium could hinder the clearing of smoke.[29] This argument indicated that even as codes were being established, their interpretation was also being developed by persons beyond such official groups as the BOCA committee, allowing competing articulations of expertise and experience. "Fragmented and ill-digested" information opened a space for negotiation and hence a space of innovation, not just for architecture, but also for the way in which fire safety science could develop.

Significantly, this process of continual negotiation was registered in the codes themselves. In the midst of paragraphs stipulating its requirements, the Basic Building Code appeared to suspend its raison d'être as a compliance document with the following statement: "Any other approved design which will achieve the same level of smoke control as described in this section may be used in lieu of these requirements."[30] This seemingly innocuous sentence, amidst a range of prescriptive statements, embedded the concept of "equivalency" within the code, that is, an allowance for different compliance solutions in response to conditions not covered by the code.[31] As was the case with Portman's Hyatt Regency Atlanta, this had been the approach, de facto, from the initial emergence of atrium buildings. One of the first articles on the subject of atriums and fire safety, published in 1974, was a case study of Florida's Disney World complex, in which Welton Becket's ziggurat-shaped Contemporary Resort hotel (1971) had a giant atrium as the centerpiece.[32] An entirely new fire code was written for the complex, and based on that experience, fire code consultant Rolf Jensen called for a shift toward a "systems-concept approach [which] normally requires the system's designers to work cooperatively with the building code and fire department officials early in the design program."[33] Another early example was Raymond Moriyama's Scarborough Civic Centre in Canada (1973), where systems to ensure the fire safety of a large public atrium were agreed between the architect, the regulators, and the local fire authority.[34] These examples show that regulation was beginning to shift away from prescriptive statements and fixed sets of dimensions and materials. Instead, equivalency could be established via the performance of spaces, materials, and mechanical systems working, as one code consultant described it, "in the aggregate."[35]

While it might appear that these changes were an inevitable development in the nature of fire safety regulation, the result of design innovation and technological development, it is important to understand them in social and political terms, as Vincent Brannigan has argued.[36] He has posited that prescriptive regulation conventionally resulted from collectively

Figure 2.6 Contemporary Resort, Disney World, Florida. Welton Becket & Associates, 1971. Bettmann Collection / Getty Images.

ratified decisions that determined acceptable levels of safety. Prescriptive regulations supported the public function of standards. However, the mid-1970s regulatory reform movement in the United States introduced the idea of variation and validation into code provisions by allowing for the equivalency of alternative solutions. Further, Brannigan has suggested that technological advancement shifted the social goals of regulation away from agreed values toward those concerned with a certain kind of freedom and the profit that could be derived from it. At the same time, the social goals of safety became technical ones met via validation rather than enforcement: "The fundamental drive was a promise of cost reduction or architectural freedom."[37]

The discussion amongst fire safety experts shows that this shift toward the equivalency of alternative solutions highlighted an emerging kind of expertise: that of the technically trained professionals who occasioned the discussion and were able to validate themselves. Yet the problem revealed by the discord amongst them is that fire safety is not technically verifiable in the same way structural safety is. As Brannigan has put it: "There is no fire safety unit really comparable to pounds per square foot of load."[38] Even so, the burgeoning field of fire safety science was beginning to show that there were redundancies and errors in measures stipulated by prescriptive codes, and this became one of the main drivers for the development of what became known as performance-based codes.[39]

By the mid-1990s, the US National Fire Prevention Association (NFPA) was making plans to implement such codes. This implementation was to be systematic and evidence-based, going beyond what were thought to be the "rather vague"[40] equivalency provisions ratified in the early 1980s. Equivalency was a way of dealing with a unique or unusual building or spatial condition, the atrium being a prime example of this. The specification of performance, on the other hand, reframed the entire approach to fire safety. In the end, the NFPA would operate a "dual track" system, whereby designers could choose to engage with prescriptive or performance-based requirements. This approach was to be implemented with the intent of

Figure 2.7 Scarborough Civic Centre, Scarborough, Canada. Raymond Moriyama, 1973. Toronto Star Collection / Getty Images.

offering a research-based lens on prescriptive practices: "a single [code] document will help direct research efforts aimed at further developing and refining calculation methods and will encourage existing prescriptive requirements to be based more on science and technology."[41] Brannigan has shown that this type of research was undertaken through modeling increasingly specific scenarios of fire behavior that were tuned to improving technical accuracy, and he has argued that this effectively led to a situation of self-regulation, whereby engineers, rather than regulators, would set all parameters for modeling performance that would then be deemed acceptable.[42] Codes, then, we to be in the service of technical development and professional positioning, not the other way around.

★★★

Despite several atrium buildings being on drawings boards and under construction in London by the early 1980s, there was no explicit recognition of the atrium in the London Building Acts, the legislative instrument that incorporated building codes. In 1980 the Greater London Council (GLC), the body responsible for code enforcement for buildings in inner London, had issued what it called an "Internal Divisional Memorandum" on atrium buildings. The memo stipulated what became known as the "sterile tube" approach,[43] which treated the atrium more like an open court, that is, essentially part of the outside of the building. As technical editor of the *Architects' Journal* Anthony Ferguson noted: "The atrium was to contain no combustible materials or fire risk activities and was separated from the adjoining office levels by walls built to the same standard as the exterior one."[44] London's first office building with an atrium, Coutts Bank on the Strand (1978), set this "sterile" standard.[45] It was a renovation of three existing nineteenth-century buildings that converged on a wedge-shaped site, a four-story atrium created out of what had once been an open court between the buildings. Rather than a world of mixed-use activities, the atrium was simply an oversized bank lobby. In 1985 the GLC updated its guidance on atriums by publishing "Fire Safety for the Atrium: Technical Information Note,"[46] which allowed for more active uses of the atrium consequent upon what it called an "engineering design approach."[47] Yet, by 1990, architect and atrium expert Richard Saxon would suggest: "The history of atrium developments in the UK is littered with places made less interesting, and more expensive, than their North American models because our regulators had different expectations."[48]

These "different expectations" arose from within an entirely different regulatory system. Shifting focus to the United Kingdom allows us to see how this system underwent wholesale change through the 1980s as a result of the deregulation agenda of Conservative Prime Minister Margaret Thatcher. The atrium again manifests these changes as they impacted life safety regulation and the knowledge and expertise generated around it. It also points to more fundamental effects of deregulation that emerged at this time. New business opportunities were opening for the profession of architecture, which was effectively deregulated in the early 1980s due to recommendations made by the Monopolies and Mergers Commission. Under new codes of conduct ratified by the Royal Institute of British Architects (RIBA) and the Architects' Registration Council of the United Kingdom (ARCUK), adherence to fixed fee scales would be abandoned; architects could effectively promote their services and were free to form limited liability companies and act as developers.[49] As Saxon's comment indicates, the atrium manifested the new potentials for urban development that deregulation prompted, especially in mixed-use development, and it also pointed to what could inhibit those potentials—regulation itself in the form of life safety codes. The appearance of the atrium in the United Kingdom accompanied the framing of regulation itself as a business opportunity, one fully aligned with the newly ratified business of architecture and development, a mode of practice that Portman had pioneered in the United States with the success of his atrium-anchored mixed-use developments.

Changes to regulation implemented in the United Kingdom were perhaps more fundamental due to its national, legislative basis. In the United

Figure 2.8 Coutts Bank, London. Frederick Gibberd, 1978. Architectural Press Archive / RIBA Collections.

States, the Model Building Codes had been developed and were updated by professional associations whose membership consisted of experts in building regulation. From the outset these nongovernmental associations had a crucial role to play in the way building regulation worked. Their codes were available for uptake by local governmental agencies that managed building compliance.[50] By contrast, regulatory change in the United Kingdom was a national, political project. In 1979, Michael Heseltine, Secretary of State for the Environment in Thatcher's newly elected government, announced the principles that would guide a review of building regulation: "maximum self-regulation; minimum Government interference; total self-financing; and simplicity in operation."[51] As a result of this review, a new Building Act was legislated in 1984, coming into force in England the following year. An accretive, legalistic, and prescriptive set of codes was replaced by an overarching Act that governed building regulations and their enforcement. Crucially, the new Building Act made provision for "approved documents" that would provide guidance on how compliance with building regulations could be achieved. These documents effectively shifted what had been the detail of prior prescriptive regulations to the status of guidance and created a performance-based approach to compliance, the approved documents allowing alternative ways to achieve it. While verification of compliance would normally sit with the relevant local authority, the new Act made provision for "approved inspectors," authorized individuals or bodies that could legally verify compliance. This opened the way for privatization and competition in building regulation.[52]

As part of the broader deregulation push to embed competition in building regulation, further change in the structure of local government was announced in 1983 in a white paper entitled "Streamlining the Cities."[53] It would lead to the GLC's becoming defunct by 1986, with London coming under the purview of the new national building legislation and regulations being enforced by local councils.[54] The atrium was again a key indicator of the scale of this shift. The GLC's technical note from 1985 was the only guidance on atrium fire safety available in the United Kingdom at that time, and fire consultant Alan Porter remarked: "As the London Building Acts have been substantially emasculated this guide is effectively obsolete."[55] Ferguson wrote that without any guidance on the kinds of risks atrium buildings posed, "we can presumably expect some very large open atrium offices without sprinklers unless insurance companies, funding institutions or local acts determine otherwise."[56]

By 1990, a suite of guides would be published in the United Kingdom by the London District Surveyors Association (LDSA), the British Standards Institution, and the Loss Prevention Council.[57] Each document reflected the professional remit of the bodies that issued it. The LDSA guidance was limited to office buildings, the Loss Prevention Council's publication was intended for insurers and underwriters, and the British Standard Code of Practice, while broadly applicable, remained in draft until it was published in final form in 1997. The differences between each reflected the increased complexity regarding who had an "interest" in fire safety, and how that interest, be it regulatory, risk-based, or design-based, was articulated.

The gap between regulatory change and the appearance of reliable guidance pointed to a problem of knowledge and expertise. With the dissolution of the GLC and the path opened for professional competition in building certification, expertise was shed from the public bodies that enforced building codes. The GLC had had a Scientific Services Branch that provided technical advice regarding building performance and regulation. The branch had a long history, emerging through the public health initiatives of the Metropolitan Board of Works in the nineteenth century.[58] Together with the GLC's Technical Policy Division, the Scientific Services Branch was vital in providing feedback and on-site testing for building performance that could underpin the development of new regulations and standards, as the building holdings of local authorities, including the GLC, were enormous. This reservoir of applied knowledge had been completely ignored in the push toward deregulation, with "Streamlining the Cities" making "no reference to the need for any technical back-up to local authority trading standards and building control activities."[59] Upon the GLC's dissolution, the Scientific Services Branch was privatized as London Scientific Services which was itself dissolved in the late 1980s.

The shifting dynamic from the public to the private was even more pronounced in the context of what had been nationally funded fire research, which had been established in the United Kingdom in 1935 with a physical testing facility at Borehamwood. What became the Fire Research Station was transferred to the Department of the Environment (as part of the Home Office) in 1971, and formally became part of the Building Research Establishment (BRE), then known as the Building Research Station, in 1972.[60] In the mid-1980s, the BRE pioneered a public-private research partnership into fire and smoke behavior in atrium buildings together with engineering consultancy Colt International (UK) Ltd. The BRE's Howard Morgan, who had authored fire safety guidance on shopping malls,[61] and Colt International's Graham Hansell staked a claim for the scientific necessity of their research program with the assertion that then-current understandings of smoke behavior and smoke control in atriums were qualitative or based on simple models, citing the published work of familiar figures in the fire code debate on both sides of the Atlantic: DeCicco, Degenkolb, Parnell, and Saxon.[62] Moving beyond these methods, the aim of the research was to provide a "fire engineering" approach that could form the basis of future guidance of direct relevance for engineers and smoke ventilation specialists.[63] Hansell and Morgan wrote: "[The research] is not intended to be a design guide for building designers. It is an attempt to derive usable design formulae for fire engineers, assembled into an overall algorithm for eventual simplification into a design guide."[64]

As was the case with research in the United States, in the United Kingdom fire safety came to be understood as the operation of engineered systems designed as a technical response to a building's program, materials, and morphology. And when the approach to safety moved beyond the architectural rules of thumb that marked earlier code discussions, the fire specialist became the researcher, the audience for the outcomes of that research, and, eventually, the certifier who would be able to validate performance-based solutions. What is notable, however, is that this research program did not immediately translate into available guidance.[65] It was not until 1994 that Hansell and Morgan published a comprehensive report and design guide under the auspices of the BRE as the culmination of their project.[66] By then, however, the public-private research partnership meant that the project's methods and findings were already being transferred into practice. Guidance, then, was an outcome of a shift to competition in building certification, rather than the basis on which that competition might be established. Research partnerships such as the one between the BRE and Colt International became a means for private firms to leverage an advantage in this arena.

Maintaining levels of funding was clearly an aim of such partnerships, with commentators remarking on the decline in public funding for fire safety research.[67] The BRE and Colt International's research program would be followed by more public-private partnerships through the 1990s. Colt International would continue atrium research together with the BRE and Arup.[68] Rosehaugh Stanhope Developments, again with Arup, funded a project to design and test new sprinkler systems for atriums, with the LSDA and the Loss Prevention Council involved in testing based on the research.[69] Fire engineering firms would also establish internal research and development units to undertake simulation and modeling. One report discussed the establishment of the Environmental Systems Department within building engineering firm Roger Preston & Partners. The department acted "as a consultancy within the consultancy," underpinning "some of the building design opportunities that are opening up."[70] At the same time as new professional services were being developed, the regulatory context for the recognition and embedding of those services was being aligned with this privatized model. Technical editor of the *Architects' Journal* Barrie Evans remarked in the mid-1990s that "researchers are working toward a more standard, accepted format for fire-engineering design guidance and regulation, one that can be worked to by designers and control authorities alike."[71] As Ross has argued, this constituted a shift in regulation from the "nominally accountable arena of legislation, to the private context of design consultation."[72]

Arup was a significant player in this privatized regulatory market. Having previously worked at the Fire Research Station, prominent fire engineer Margaret Law established Arup's fire safety division.[73] Arup pioneered an engineering approach to fire safety in Gateway Two (1983), the headquarters designed by their architecture division, Arup Associates, for paper company Wiggins Teape, situated in the office park environment of Basingstoke outside London. Five floors of naturally ventilated office accommodation were arranged around a top-lit atrium. Due to then-current fire code restrictions, the atrium was only to be used during office hours for circulation; however, Arup Associates obtained a building regulation waiver allowing other social uses outside of hours, such as staff playing badminton and putting on dinners. These possibilities for the active use of the atrium meant that the building became a key example visited by fire officers.[74] Arup would move onto offering what they called "total design"[75] services that extended to the technical verification of building designs, perhaps most significantly with their modeling of smoke behavior in the atrium of Richard Rogers Partnership's Lloyd's of London building (1986).[76] The design positioned the insurance market's famous underwriting room at the core of a twelve-story atrium, its spatial flexibility deployed as a form of insurance against the unknowable future demands of the industry.[77]

The role of expertise available on a consultative basis became firmly entrenched across the research-regulation apparatus. Research partnerships emerged as the mechanism by which experts would increase knowledge, provide guidance on life safety, and certify performance-based solutions, all in the name of innovation, that is, a market-led approach to the way knowledge could develop and be applied in pursuit of efficient, competitive, and novel business opportunities. Indeed, Ross has argued that because of Arup's ability to offer its "total design" expertise internationally has meant that the firm has taken on, de facto, a global regulatory role. Since the 2000s Arup has continued to refine the dynamic, computational

Figure 2.9 Gateway Two, Basingstoke, United Kingdom. Arup Associates, 1983. Architectural Press Archive / RIBA Collections.

Figure 2.10 Lloyd's of London, London. Richard Rogers Partnership, 1986. Alastair Hunter / RIBA Collections.

modeling of fire behavior to "disprove" the idea that compartmentation in a building necessarily inhibits the spread of fire, or that large volumes such as atriums pose an increased safety risk.[78] As a result, atriums have continued to proliferate as a material instantiation of deregulation.

★★★

Despite the increasing transfer of knowledge and expertise to the private sector, in the United Kingdom local councils were still authorized to certify building safety under the national legislation. Their authority, however, had been significantly undermined. A final example illustrates what happened to local authority certification after deregulation, and what that meant for the role of the architect. In 1986 architect Ray Moxley broke ground on Chelsea Harbour, a seventeen-building mixed-use development on the banks of the River Thames in West London, introducing a style of development as close to Portman's as the United Kingdom had seen. The development featured luxury housing, a hotel, a marina, and two atrium buildings. One accommodated a commercial design center under three enormous, glazed domes. The other, Harbour Yard, was proposed with a mix of uses unique in the United Kingdom at the time: apartments, offices, commercial studios, and restaurants. As an architect at the head of a development consortium, Moxley had pioneered an approach to design and construction that became known as fast building, and Chelsea Harbour's rapid construction—it was completed in just two and a half years—demonstrated his aim that the architect should take charge of all aspects of the design, development, and construction process.[79]

Writing about the Harbour Yard building part way through Chelsea Harbour's construction, Brian Finnimore, the design coordinator in charge of the development, outlined a series of interdependencies as well as frictions between architecture, now fully unleashed as a competitive, commercially oriented profession, and the residual structure of building regulation:

> It is the speed with which modern buildings are constructed that most exposes the deficiencies in the present system. As with many other schemes, Chelsea Harbour was built on a "fast track" approach using a "construction management" type of building contract. Under this system the design is finalized and fully negotiated with the local authority well after building work begins on site. To accelerate construction speed the building process is split into a series of different packages related to the work of the different specialist contractors. The commencement of each package is timed in order to achieve the fastest overall completion of the project. The detailed design information is prepared to suit this sequence of packages. Therefore, construction of the structural frame begins on the basis of a set of broad assumptions on the final plan of the building—quite possibly the day after planning consent has been granted. It is, therefore, important that these assumptions are accurate to avoid costly structural alterations later on. However, these assumptions cannot at present be relied upon as there is no firm basis for the design of atria in relation to one of their most important aspects—fire safety.[80]

The design and construction of Harbour Yard's atrium brought to the fore the consequences of the performance-based approach governed by the new Building Act. Perhaps counterintuitively in the context of the opening up of regulation and certification, Finnimore's plea was for a strong statutory code for fire safety in atriums in order to ensure certainty in the design and construction process. Yet none was forthcoming, and what Finnimore was being forced to recognize, to his evident chagrin, was that in a situation of rapid construction—the aim of another of Heseltine's regulatory reforms[81]—the architect had to make decisions that would balance risk and reward. It was up to the architect to procure the right kind of advice, or to proceed with certain assumptions regarding whether a design would eventually be deemed safe. Engaging a consultant engineer could well delay a project and have significant financial consequences. In the end, such concerns did not delay the successful completion of Harbour Yard.

It is a particular feature of neoliberalism that a position of increased risk becomes one of increased reward. In the case of Chelsea Harbour, the reward was clearly financial. The reduced construction time meant a shorter period of financial exposure and an asset more quickly released to the market. Success in this instance meant that the architect—Moxley as architect-developer—could demonstrate how risk was actively and successfully managed. The atrium buildings at Chelsea Harbour effectively made risk tolerance the centerpiece of professional competence. And as the underwriters who dwelt at the base of Lloyd's' atrium knew only too well, the insurance industry only existed because risk itself was a financial product.

The consequence of an architect arguing that an atrium should be "just part of the building" was that the architect should also be willing to take on the risk involved in such a claim, regulation becoming an apparatus that promoted risk as a professional opportunity. To be sure, the upheavals in regulation did create the conditions for new, technical knowledge to develop regarding the fire safety of atrium buildings, primarily that of the engineer and code specialist. Where once equivalency provisions as exceptions to a prescriptive code had allowed different professions to work together to solve the problems of a novel spatial condition, the increasingly embedded performance basis of regulation meant that professional opportunity had become an end in itself, with architects, engineers, and certifiers each making their own, specific calculations as to where the opportunities for profit and loss lay.

3

Conditioning

Putting a lid on an open court creates an atrium, that is, a separate, bounded, quasi-exterior environment within a building, and some characteristics of that environment can be defined and measured. Cambridge researcher Dean Hawkes and architect Richard MacCormac teamed up to study what this meant for a discipline and profession trying to grapple with the aftermath of the energy crisis. In the late 1970s they designed a model office building that put a glazed roof over a set of Leslie Martin and Lionel March's non-prismatic court forms. In its simplest, cellular form, a perimeter band of office space surrounded an atrium that was naturally ventilated. These cells could be multiplied and aggregated together in a variety of ways to form a building. Hawkes and MacCormac characterized the atriums of these potential buildings as "ambiguous inside/outside spaces" that supported "the convivial activities of the city."[1]

The text accompanying the publication of the model office building outlined a set of calculations to demonstrate that in the climatic conditions in the United Kingdom, the design, depending on its final form, could reduce energy consumption to around half of that of a standard, air-conditioned office building. The atrium conserved energy by reducing the conductive heat loss from its surrounding built volumes. For the purposes

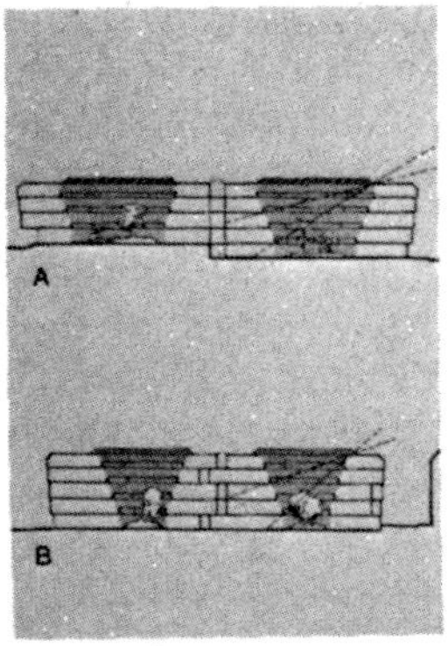

11 Urban study: sections

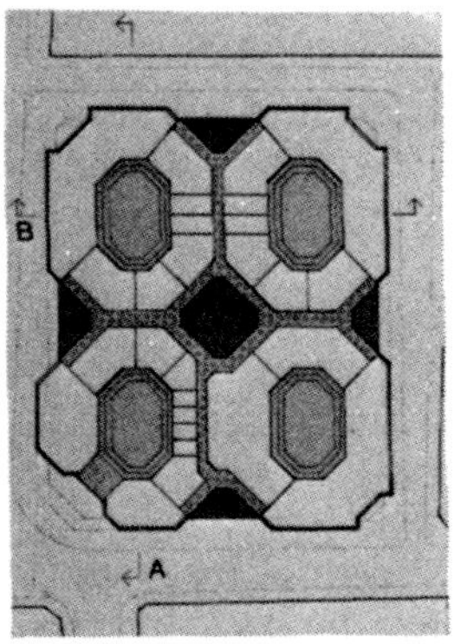

12 Urban study: plan

13 Urban office court interior

Figure 3.1 Model Office Design, shown in urban configuration. Dean Hawkes and Richard MacCormac. Source: *RIBA Journal* 85, no. 6 (June 1978): 246. Courtesy Dean Hawkes, MJP Architects, and RIBA Publications.

of calculating energy performance, the atrium was considered part of the external environment. As Hawkes explained: "The effect is to increase substantially the 'external' design temperature which is assumed for heat loss calculations. A further advantage is that the glazed space is habitable for much of the year without the need for supplementary heating."[2] The atrium effectively acted as a heat storage unit, moderating the climatic conditions that impacted the buildings's energy consumption.

But it was the use of the term "ambiguous" to describe the atrium—Hawkes would also refer to the atrium's "indeterminacy"[3]—that was perhaps most significant. The atrium was neither inside nor outside. It could be used in ways not normally considered in office planning. This gave the impetus for a new understanding of the relationship between energy performance and built form, one that also raised significant questions: The atrium's energy benefits could be projected based on abstract calculations and model designs, but how would an atrium perform once built? Adjustable environmental control could be offered in place of air-conditioning, but would a building's inhabitants feel comfortable, or be able to effectively adapt—and adapt to—the indoor environment of an atrium building? And what did it really mean to feel "comfortable" in the workplace?

Ambiguity and indeterminacy also stemmed from the broader context. The availability and stability of energy supplies was increasingly in doubt. Some energy reduction strategies significantly reduced ventilation levels and contributed to sick building syndrome. With its multiple symptoms and no discernible underlying cause, sick building syndrome was the most uncertain of occupational health concerns, signaling what Michelle Murphy has characterized as "a confusion of boundaries between buildings and the bodies in them."[4]

Hawkes and MacCormac's design crystallized a set of concerns that would extend into the 1980s and '90s regarding architecture, its energy performance, and the kind of indoor environment it produced. As a material condition, the atrium stimulated new, integrated ways to calculate and design for better thermal performance, and to consider different kinds of occupancy and use at the center of those techniques. Research programs emerged and became increasingly focused on the development of sophisticated models of performance and on the analysis of case studies. And guidance was produced for architects about the principles and design techniques that could be used to enhance an atrium's energy performance.

The atrium's indeterminacy would be a key driver in these approaches. As rigid conceptions of comfort tied to thermal stability were seen to contribute to inefficient and unhealthy buildings, the potential for variability in the atrium's performance helped loosen the hold air-conditioning had on the production of habitable indoor environments. The atrium enabled architects to integrate the variables that constituted its indoor environment, and, in so doing, to demonstrate their professional expertise. It also gave this integration a striking spatial figure, one that would be advanced as a symbol of how buildings could be healthier and more environmentally responsible.

★★★

Before the atrium began to blur rigid distinctions between inside and outside, these distinctions were strengthened with the advent of air-conditioning in the twentieth century. While it rapidly became associated with cooling, air-conditioning was initially developed to control humidity.[5] The American Society of Heating and Ventilation Engineers (ASHVE) established a laboratory in Pittsburgh in 1919, funded by the US Bureau of Mines, to research indoor climate. Laboratories were also established at Harvard and Yale universities.[6] This research directly aided the burgeoning air-conditioning industry by providing accurate, quantitative measurements of key variables that constituted the indoor environment: air temperature, air movement, and humidity. The focus was on human comfort and the way in which the effects of these variables were registered as the so-called "skin effects" of indoor climate.[7]

Ventilation became one of the main battlegrounds in the rise of air-conditioning. Since the early nineteenth century, fresh-air ventilation had been a concern in ensuring buildings had safe, habitable environments. While mechanical ventilation had existed prior to air-conditioning and had been necessitated in large indoor spaces such as theaters and auditoriums, the emergence of air-conditioning offered a different kind of environmental control. Backed by their belief in the emerging science that governed their technology, in the 1920s ASHVE opposed the idea that fresh-air ventilation should be achieved by the permeability of a building's fabric.[8] It was not only that external air, especially in urban areas, could be deemed unsafe or far from fresh.[9] Rather, an artificially produced indoor climate could be measured, and its variables more easily controlled. In place of health, comfort became the prime goal of air-conditioning because it could be conceptualized and achieved technically by an optimum zone, a "comfort zone" framed by temperature, humidity, and airflow.[10]

The increasing dominance of air-conditioning in the debate on ventilation would see ASHVE remove "ventilation" from its name, changing it to the American Society of Heating and Air-Conditioning Engineers (ASHAE) in 1954. Five years later it would merge with the American Society of Refrigeration Engineers (ASRE) to form the American Society of Heating, Refrigeration and Air-Conditioning Engineers (ASHRAE). Even though ventilation was expunged from the professional association's name, this merger would promote heating, ventilation, and air-conditioning (HVAC) systems as the means to standardize and control the indoor environment.[11] This standardization continued to be underpinned by extensive research, as ASHRAE moved its Pittsburgh laboratory to Kansas State University in 1963 and began receiving funding from the US Department of Defense as the applicability of sealed, controlled interior environments became crucial to both the space race and the Cold War.[12] Working there and later at the Technical University of Denmark, Povl Ole Fanger would pioneer calculations that combined temperature, humidity, and airflow with human metabolic rate and with the effects of insulation provided by clothing. These inputs produced Fanger's comfort equation and predicted mean vote (PMV). The comfort equation enabled these variables to be calculated so as to achieve an environment of thermal comfort. PMV worked in the other direction, correlating a prediction of the average vote of a large group of people regarding their perception of comfort with the range of calculated variables.[13] Fanger's equations underpinned successive versions of ASHRAE Standard 55, "Thermal Environmental Conditions for Human Occupancy," which was first released in 1966 and updated at the beginning of the 1970s, '80s, and '90s.[14] The standard introduced a definition of comfort that was taken up by Fanger:

> Thermal comfort for a person is here defined as "that condition of mind which expresses satisfaction with the thermal environment." If a group of people is subject to the same room climate, it will not be possible, due to biological variance, to satisfy everyone at the same time. One must then aim at creating optimal thermal comfort for the group, i.e., a condition in which the highest possible percentage of the group is in thermal comfort.[15]

Since the establishment of research programs on the indoor environment, this "person" whose comfort stood in for "the group" was white, male, college-age, and middle-class.[16] He was the experimental subject whose "skin effects" and metabolism were measured in labs, and whose sedentary working conditions were the focus for achieving a "comfortable" indoor climate, "a neutral atmosphere that least exerted itself on bodies in business dress"[17] and that sealed off those bodies from the threats and variability of the outside.[18]

With the rise of air-conditioning and its backing by quantitative research, the architectural knowledge that had developed in the first half of the twentieth century to control the thermal properties inside buildings via facade treatments began to fall away. Brise-soleils and other screening devices, not to mention openable windows, were progressively stripped from the lexicon of modern architecture. Daniel Barber has captured this dynamic between the architectural and mechanical control of climate, from materially modulated variability to mechanical control for a universal climate:

> The conceptualization of the thermal interior initially developed through careful coordination between design elements, knowledge of climatic patterns, and assumptions about inhabitants' resilient capacity to adjust to different thermal conditions; this same aspiration for achieving thermal balance was then integrated into mechanical systems, modeling processes, and regulatory structures that, by contrast, were seen to be universal and everywhere applicable, able to produce an identical climate anywhere and across time.[19]

In the mid-1950s, it was claimed that almost every new significant office building constructed in North America since the end of the Second World War incorporated air-conditioning, with the sealed, glazed box predominating.[20] Because of the cheap and plentiful power available through the 1960s, one expert noted that it was usual for the temperature in office buildings on the East Coast of the United States to be maintained at 24 degrees Celsius, 24 hours a day, each day of the year.[21]

Of course, this assumption of mechanically powered climatic universality enabled by air-conditioning was severely tested with the energy crisis of 1973. As fuel prices skyrocketed, increasing up to tenfold during the 1970s,[22] there was immediate pressure to reduce the energy consumption of buildings, which had, on average, risen twofold per square foot for office buildings in the United States between 1950 and 1970.[23] Again ventilation was an area of concern, as it had a major influence on temperature variation and the energy used to regulate it.

As a result of a new ventilation standard released in 1981, air change rates in buildings fell between 30% and 50% to levels not seen since their initial introduction in the early nineteenth century.[24] ASHRAE, which had developed the new standard, was also involved in wider efforts to codify energy reduction strategies for buildings, including a new standard developed in 1980 together with the Illuminating Engineering Society (IES) and the American National Standards Institute (ANSI). This standard sought to reduce energy consumption in all new buildings by an estimated 40%.[25] For existing buildings, ASHRAE revised its Standard 55 to specify a wider range of indoor temperatures as being acceptable for comfort.[26]

Such efforts, though, produced a new set of problems. Existing buildings were often hastily retrofitted with insulation and the levels of external ventilation through building facades by "involuntary infiltration" were reduced.[27] While this mostly occurred in residential buildings, in office buildings in particular HVAC systems could be thrown off balance by these measures as new feedback entered the system. Unforeseen effects such as moisture buildup could occur, causing condensation, corrosion, and other safety concerns in building fabric.[28] Buildings were becoming even more tightly sealed, with HVAC systems working beyond the parameters for which they were designed.

The combined effects of these changes on the indoor environment contributed to what became known as sick building syndrome, described by one expert as "complaints of eye irritation, headaches, dizziness, fever, nausea, sleepiness, and poor concentration for every segment of the population and every type of building."[29] These effects were first made evident in 1976 in several government and educational buildings in North America, leading to building closures over subsequent years and hundreds of complaints investigated in the United States by the National Institute for Occupational Safety and Health (NIOSH), the Centers for Disease Control (CDC), and the Environmental Protection Agency (EPA).[30] While decreased rates of ventilation consequent upon energy restrictions and retrofitting were identified as a prime factor in the rise of sick building syndrome, a range of further contributing factors was associated with it, including contaminants and odors emanating from building and furnishing materials as well as from humans themselves, temperature and humidity variations, the socio-psychological condition of building occupants including levels of satisfaction or stress, and the operation and maintenance of buildings' infrastructure including lighting and HVAC systems. The complex interaction of these factors led two commentators to a definition that captured the indeterminacy of sick building syndrome: "If there is no clearly identifiable cause, and symptoms diminish or disappear after occupants leave the building, the problem is often called 'sick building syndrome.'"[31] At the same time, knowledge was increasing about the nature and range of indoor pollutants, prime among them being asbestos, radon, formaldehyde, and tobacco smoke.[32]

It was not simply that indoor air was more polluted and therefore needed amelioration. The pursuit of comfort created stable, homogenous environments that were supposed to exclude all that was thought to be dangerous. But the ability to measure and control air quality with increasing sophistication led to the identification of potentially hazardous chemicals within the presumably safe interior. As one expert put it: "our knowledge of air pollutants is distorted by the availability of analytical techniques: we tend to ignore problems until we can measure them accurately, but tend to overreact to and worry about potential effects of anything that we can measure and express in numbers."[33]

While indoor air quality could be accurately measured in terms of some variables—indeed, such an ability to measure gave rise to the very idea of indoor air quality—office interiors were not labs. Sick building syndrome evaded quantitative measurement and causative reasoning, its effects being felt most strongly by women office workers. As one commentator expressed it, sick building syndrome presented not as discomfort but something much less measurable, "a dissatisfaction with the environment."[34] NIOSH psychologists even thought that it could be an example of mass psychogenic illness amongst women office workers.[35] "Human perception" had entered an arena dominated by quantitative thinking. The response from the HVAC industry was perhaps predictable: users of buildings were contributing to their "perceived" illnesses.[36] As one commentator saw it, "For air-conditioned buildings air tightness is more of a psychological factor, occupants seeing the building as a hermetic, and therefore oppressive, environment,"[37] and "a discontented workforce may be more disposed to blame the environment."[38] Another identified "general dissatisfaction and psychosomatic"[39] factors as being significant. One researcher went so far as to suggest: "Human error is the major cause of 'sick' buildings. People forget to plug in a computer that controls ventilation, do not continuously run the ventilation system when the building opens in order to save a few dollars, block the air intake with plantings, misuse and abuse equipment, and do many other things than can undermine even the best design." He then added, without irony: "There have already been so many human-factor problems in new tight [i.e., sealed] buildings that one has to question this society's ability to manage complex, computer-controlled heating, air conditioning and ventilation systems."[40]

Regulation, too, was blamed. No single agency was responsible for monitoring and regulating indoor air quality in the United States. Instead, a mix of five agencies were involved due to the complex contributing factors. These included the Occupational Health and Safety Administration (OHSA), the Department of Housing and Urban Development (HUD), the Consumer Product Safety Commission (CPSC), as well as the EPA and the Department of Energy (DOE). Even as they worked together toward defining standards for indoor air quality, the EPA and the DOE were at loggerheads; the DOE was concerned that indoor air quality could be compromised by tighter energy standards.[41] In a similar fashion, the aims of ASHRAE's energy reduction and ventilation standards were seen to conflict with one another.[42] Perhaps surprisingly, research into—and the promotion of the idea of—sick building syndrome was spearheaded by the tobacco industry. As Murphy recounts, in 1988 the industry set up the nonprofit Center for Indoor Air Research "which quickly became the largest nongovernmental source of funding for indoor air pollution research . . . tobacco companies [hoping] that the plethora of products contributing to indoor pollution would help take the spotlight off cigarettes."[43] In the absence of a cause, and with nonspecific symptoms, the concept of sick building syndrome meant that the regulation of indoor air might be avoided altogether.

A federal Indoor Air Quality Act was passed into law in the United States in 1991, and the white, male, middle-class body that was the subject of the comfortable, sealed, lab-tested interior had become so ubiquitous in standards, norms, and technologies as to disappear. As Murphy has shown, what reemerged in his place was an imperiled body belonging primarily to women office workers whose claims regarding illness were treated, at best, with suspicion.[44] They would have to resort to their own grassroots efforts to have the effects of sick building syndrome recognized and taken seriously, producing new forms of experience-based evidence even as causation remained elusive.[45]

In all of this the billion-dollar HVAC industry remained ascendant, and the presence of HVAC systems central to how indoor air quality would continue to be tackled.[46] Building designers were being positioned as legally responsible for indoor air quality, which meant the correct specification, installation, and design for the operating environment of HVAC systems: "Builders and owners perceive architects/planners as the conductors of the design 'orchestra,' and because of this perception architects/planners are likely to be involved in lawsuits about 'sick' buildings. Industrial hygienists and other health scientists expect architects/planners and social scientists to design preventive measures into their buildings."[47]

The preventive measures that design could offer, however, were not just about the correct implementation of mechanical systems. Rather, they had the potential to address the spatial problem that underlay the rise of the sealed building and the ills it caused: the rigid distinction between inside and outside. It was the morphological and spatial possibilities inherent in the atrium that would reintroduce an architectural way of configuring the indoor environment of buildings. Where facade-based design techniques had been the primary means to manage the interior environment prior to air-conditioning, the spatial modulation the atrium provided would offer new potentials beyond the sealed building.[48]

***

Atriums could contribute to buildings' excessive energy consumption or poor health effects, if they were in sealed buildings that relied on powered environmental control. However, in the context of uncertainty over energy and building health, the atrium's spatial ambiguity offered an advantage. In lieu of a one-size-fits-all approach to standards and norms, the atrium emerged as a spatial and material condition that could be subject to testing and modulation in use. Its inherent blurring of inside and outside meant that singular energy solutions or modes of operation were rarely prescribed. Within it, the interaction between a building's energy consumption and its mode of occupation became the subject of research.

In the United Kingdom, Hawkes led the way in promoting this understanding of the atrium. In 1980, as director of the Martin Centre for Architectural and Urban Research, which had been established in 1974 as the successor to LUBFS, Hawkes organized a conference titled "The Architecture of Energy" and used it to lay out his account of the atrium and energy performance. He began by questioning the then-current maxim that energy-efficient buildings "should be large rather than small and have circular or square plans, heated buildings should be near cubical in shape, but air-conditioned buildings should be lower, depending on the amount of glazing."[49] This maxim generally relied on what Hawkes defined as the "exclusive mode" of environmental control, the use of building form and fabric "to exclude the effects of the external environment upon the internal conditions."[50] In a knowing reference to Reyner Banham's "well-tempered environment,"[51] Hawkes sought to shift away from the exclusive mode by introducing the concept of the "selective mode" of environmental control—"the admission of substantial elements of the external environment into the building."[52] He noted that such a mode had prevailed in temperate climates and that its main benefits occurred in the utilization rather than the exclusion of ambient energy—the heat and light in the immediate environment. The selective-mode building was "one in which summertime overheating is avoided by means which do not consume energy, in which solar gain is regarded as a desirable input in the heating season and in which natural lighting is seen as a major component of the environment. The discussion of the relationship between shape and energy thus begins from a completely different standpoint."[53]

One of the most spectacular illustrations of this approach was provided by Stephen Greenberg, an architect with Peter Bell & Partners, who presented at the conference two designs for hotels in London that adopted and inverted the air-conditioned atrium model popularized in the designs of John Portman. Portman's inaugural atrium hotel, the Hyatt Regency Atlanta (1967), employed an innovative gas-powered air-conditioning system that circulated three million cubic feet of air at 190,000 cubic feet per minute through its twenty-two-story atrium.[54] The designs Greenberg discussed adopted Portman's formal arrangement, but the English location presented a different set of opportunities, with a glazed roof allowing for passive heating of the atrium. The initial design concept proposed that access to the hotel rooms would be via galleries open to the atrium along the lines of the Portman model. The rooms would be heated by warmed air drawn in from the atrium, boosted by supplementary heating in each room. To mitigate heat loss through the external facade, the exterior wall would contain small window openings, with the whole structure surrounded by a further glazed skin that utilized Trombe effects. Based on advice from Cambridge University researchers, an alternative, more energy-efficient version was also developed, with the orientation of the rooms being reversed so that they would face into the atrium with access placed on the exterior of the building. This meant a lower ambient temperature in the

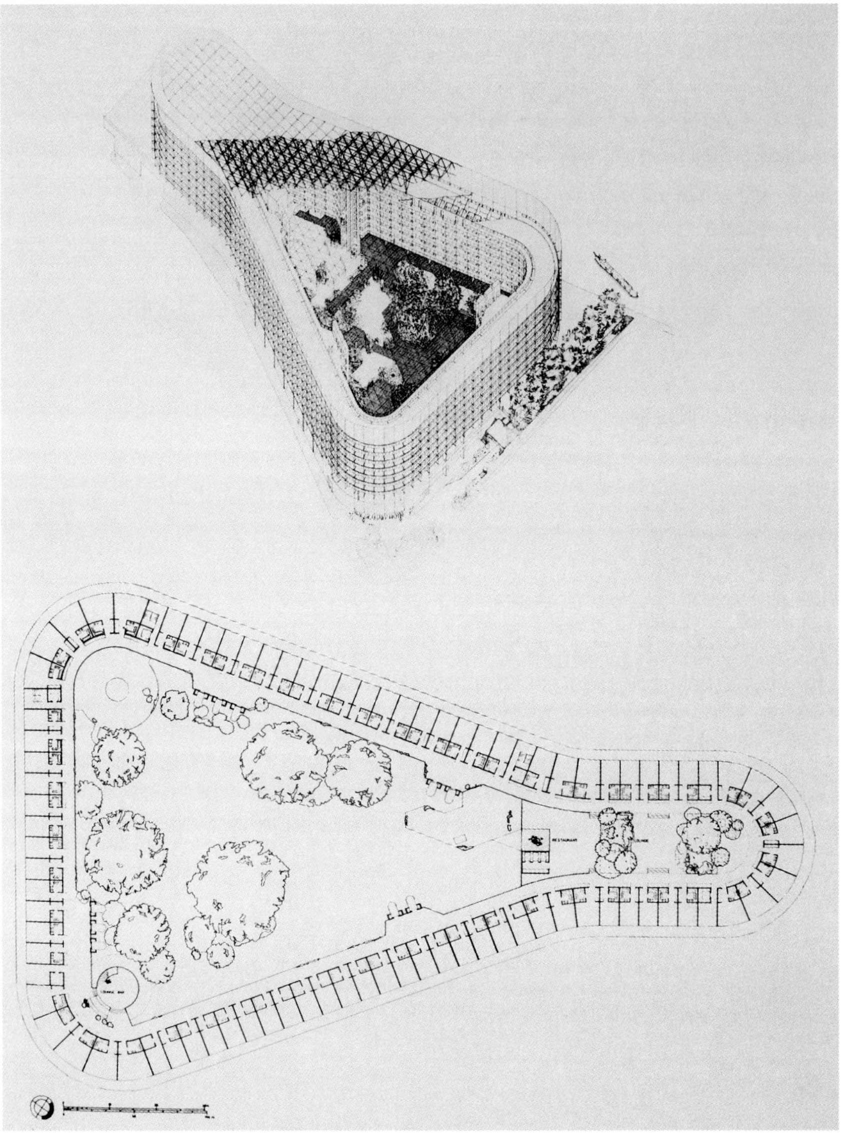

Figure 3.2 Granary Hotel, London, design proposal. Stephen Greenberg and Peter Bell. Source: Dean Hawkes and Janet Owers, eds., *The Architecture of Energy* (London: Construction Press, 1981), 183. Courtesy Stephen Greenberg and Peter Bell.

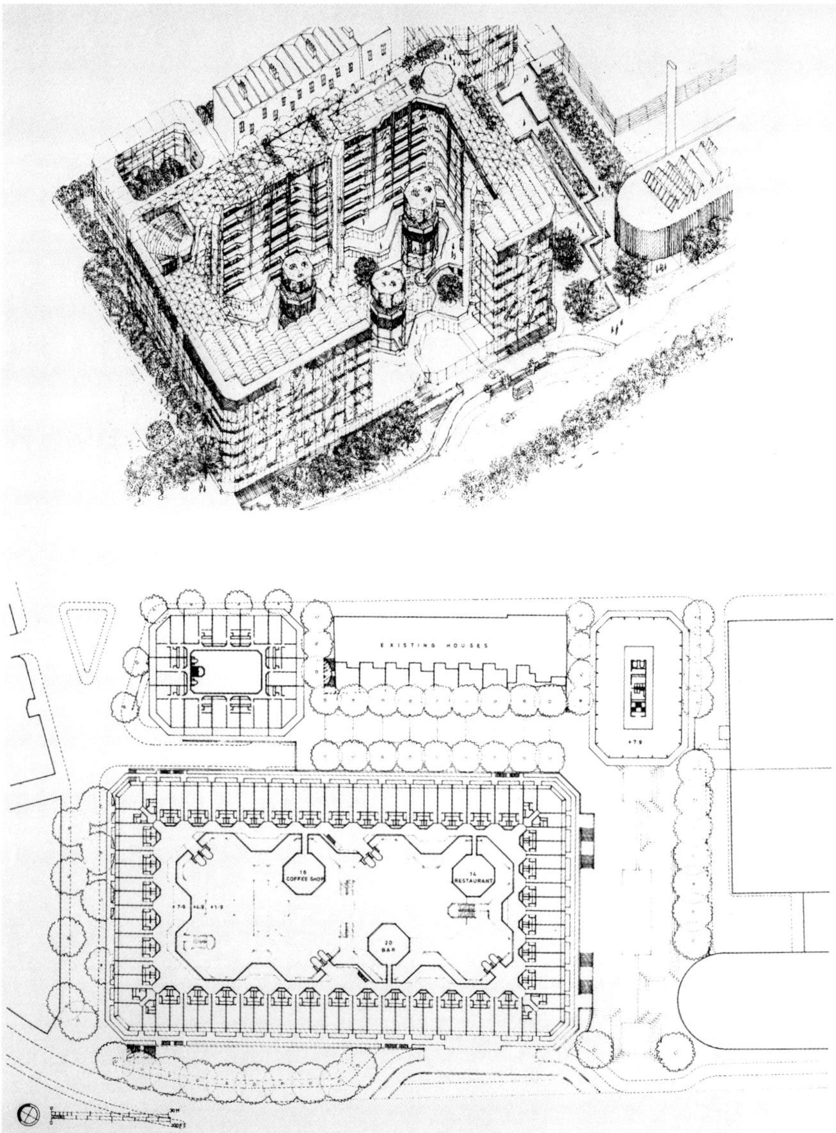

Figure 3.3 Swiss Cottage Hotel, London, design proposal. Stephen Greenberg and Peter Bell. Source: Dean Hawkes and Janet Owers, eds., *The Architecture of Energy* (London: Construction Press, 1981), 184. Courtesy Stephen Greenberg and Peter Bell.

circulation space, an increased insulating buffer to the exterior, and mitigation of heat loss from the bedrooms.[55]

Other examples of atrium buildings were presented at the conference, including Foster Associates' Willis Faber & Dumas Headquarters in Ipswich (1975)[56] and Alex Gordon's Crown Offices, Cardiff (1979),[57] and the atrium seemed to have an outsized influence on the conference. In a set of closing reflections, architect George Kasabov remarked: "As it is an architectural conference, most attention has inevitably been given to what is the appropriate *form* for energy efficient buildings. Indeed, the atrium could almost be taken as the 'leitmotif' for the whole conference."[58] Another, more guarded response was given by engineer Max Fordham, who listed a series of "useful ideas" from the conference, including "Atrium buildings can be nice"; however, the atrium also appeared on his list of "worries": "The kind of thinking which is being used to present the atrium building as attractive is not backed up by any clear evaluation of its need for energy to keep it comfortable." This comment may be related to another worry in Fordham's list: "There was a paucity of measured results to correlate with (dubious?) computer techniques."[59]

While Fordham's dismissal of emerging techniques, including computation, may seem overstated, it emphasized something significant: calculating buildings' energy performance was becoming increasingly complex and specific to particular formal and material configurations. The methods that underpinned energy calculations were based on projections, yet the evaluations of these projections in built examples were increasingly based on analysis in use, often over extended time periods. Any single model of a building's energy performance was not generalizable, and it might not be possible to obtain a close correlation between a model and the performance of a built example. As the Cambridge researchers emphasized, computer models of built forms remained distinct from material buildings.[60]

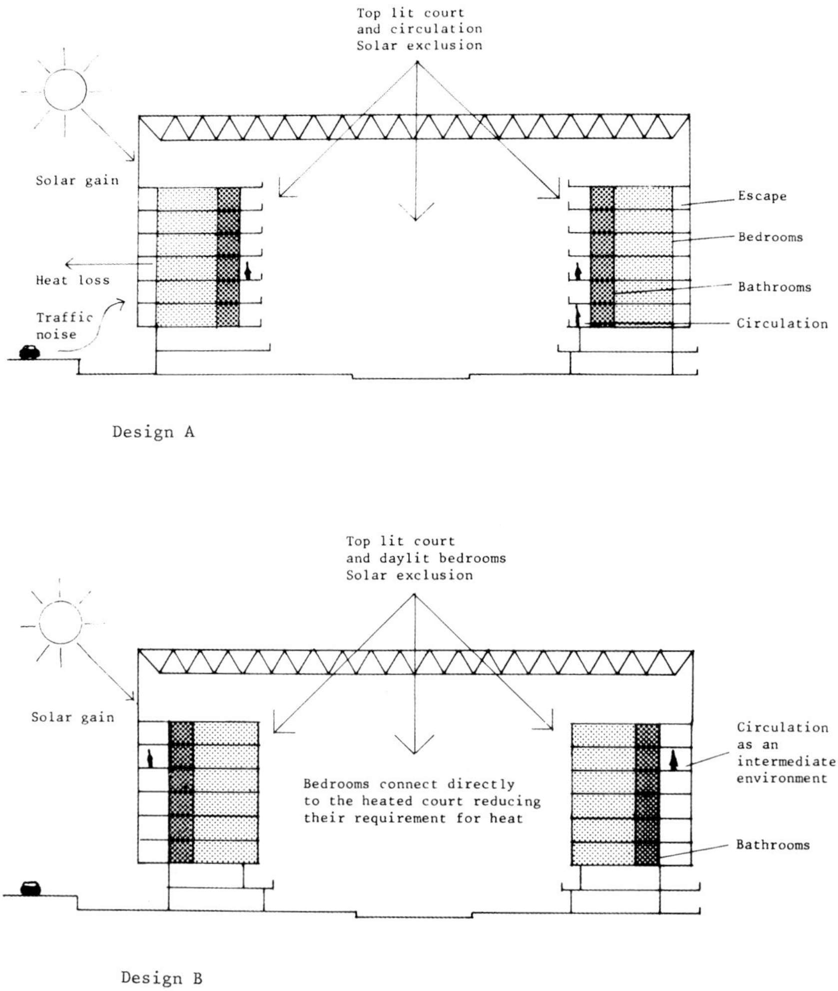

Figure 3.4 Granary Hotel and Swiss Cottage Hotel, alternative schematic designs. Stephen Greenberg and Peter Bell. Source: Dean Hawkes and Janet Owers, eds., *The Architecture of Energy* (London: Construction Press, 1981), 188. Courtesy Stephen Greenberg and Peter Bell.

Figure 3.5 Willis Faber & Dumas Headquarters, Ipswich, United Kingdom. Foster Associates, 1975. John Donat / RIBA Collections.

To attempt to bridge the gap between built forms and specific buildings, the discussion of general principles and distinctive cases in professional magazines would become an increasingly prominent channel for researchers.[61] These publications often presented highly technical research to a broader professional audience, and they were also able to draw their own insights from what they observed about the performance of buildings in use. Together with his colleague Nick Baker, Hawkes published a series of articles in the *Architects' Journal* on the topic of atriums and energy performance.[62]

The new headquarters for British Telecom in London (1984) was discussed by Hawkes as a kind of test of Cambridge's built form research.[63] The building occupied a large site in the shadow of St. Paul's Cathedral. As such, it was subject to height, massing, and plot ratio restrictions, meaning that the court form became the most efficient way for the building to occupy its deep site, the court becoming an enclosed atrium. The brief stipulated a sealed building, and fire regulations at the time prohibited the public use of the atrium. Despite this functional restriction, the atrium was left without air-conditioning, and Hawkes noted that the building asked "technical questions which, for the moment, standard environmental design prediction methods cannot answer."[64] What he meant is perhaps demonstrated by his analysis of the headquarters for the paper company Wiggins Teape, known as Gateway Two (1983), designed by Arup Associates and situated in the office park environment of Basingstoke outside London. The building took the court form, with five floors of naturally ventilated office accommodation arranged around a top-lit atrium. The facade was designed to minimize heat gain while balancing natural illumination primarily through fixed shading and thermal mass. Ventilation was enabled by the stack effect of the atrium, drawing fresh air in through the facade. Heating was provided by hot-water radiators, with the atrium containing an underfloor heating system operating at low temperature. In addition, heat generated by the company's computer facility, which ran 24 hours a day, was recycled through the atrium in winter.

Figure 3.6 British Telecom Headquarters, London. Property Services Agency, UK Department of the Environment, 1984. Jonathan Goldberg / Alamy.

In this configuration, the building's environmental performance was enabled by what Hawkes defined as "simple systems and advanced controls."[65] A group of around five hundred employees who had previously worked in a fully air-conditioned office, Gateway One (1976, known as Gateway House) also designed by Arup Associates, were now the "advanced controllers" responsible for the local modulation of their environment by means of operable windows and localized lighting, while the atrium was able to be ventilated via mechanically controlled openings. The users were also able to enjoy the atrium as a social benefit, with a waiver from the local fire authority enabling it to be used for social events outside of business hours. Hawkes thought that "demonstrable technical success"[66] had been met with similar "social success."[67]

Yet Hawkes knew that success couldn't be determined simply by observing the conditions only three months after the building had opened. He returned to Gateway Two a year later and found figures on the building's energy consumption to be "commendably low, confirming the theoretical arguments about the utility of the atrium form."[68] He noted that some retrofitting had taken place, including local air-conditioning in the restaurant, with fans and supplementary lighting in use in some offices, all of which he called "fine tuning."[69]

More significant than whether any individual design was deemed to be successful was the idea that users and their localized adjustments were beginning to be seen—and embraced—as part of the variability that marked the atrium's environmental performance. This didn't exactly answer Fordham's plea for measured results to correlate with abstract models, but it did provide some evidence about what the variability of the atrium could offer after sick building syndrome—not a cure for it, but an embrace of the kind of user intervention that some thought was a cause of the syndrome in the first place. In a contribution to Hawkes's Cambridge conference, David Fisk, who was then Head of the Mechanical and Electrical Engineering Division at the Building Research Establishment and the author of the reference work *Thermal Control of Buildings*,[70] discussed a shift away from comfort as a fixed, abstract determinant toward energy consumption as something that implied a choice largely by the building user about their own comfort. Here the idea of the selective mode took on a different kind of significance. While Hawkes's definition implied that, in some sense, it was the design, and therefore the designer, who selected, for Fisk comfort standards were those for the building user to take up. Directly critiquing Fanger, Fisk posited that such choices were social, political, and economic: "How immutable are our 'comfort standards,' especially in the context of an expensive energy future?"[71] Baker, too, would chime in with a critique of Fanger and his influence, coining the term "irritable occupant" to contend that a user's dissatisfaction with environmental conditions derived not from a stable environment being experienced as uncomfortable, but rather from the lack of an opportunity to adapt personally to what ought to be the inherently variable nature of that environment.[72]

★★★

In the context of wider climatic variance, and with the initial experience of atrium buildings as sealed and air-conditioned, an understanding of the environmental and energy benefits of the atrium emerged in the United States in the years following the energy crisis. Several built examples were covered in the professional architectural press, including the Children's Hospital of Philadelphia (1974) by Harbeson Hough Livingston & Larson, a building arranged as a U shape around a large central atrium-cum-lobby;[73] Minneapolis's Butler Square (1974) by Miller Hanson Westerbeck Bell, a retrofit of an early twentieth-century timber-framed warehouse where atriums were carved out of the existing structure in two phases, environmental performance lessons learned from the first informing the design of the subsequent renovation, in 1980, by Arvid Elness, the lead architect of the original scheme;[74] three projects by SOM, 33 West Monroe, Chicago (1980), the Pan American Life Insurance Company, New Orleans (1980), and Atrium One, Cincinnati (1981), where atriums provided amenity, lower construction costs, and energy advantages for the deep-floor-plan buildings;[75] and the Lockheed Missiles & Space Company in Sunnyvale, California (1983) by Leo A. Daly, where an east-west atrium cut through an elongated, five-story form to provide natural lighting.[76] Also prominent was the State Office Building in Sacramento, known as the Bateson Building (1981), designed by Sim Van der Ryn with Peter Calthorpe. It featured a central atrium in a four-story building with a sophisticated HVAC system that took advantage of the temperature differential between day and night, expelling warm air and using night air to cool the building. Large, sculpture-like tubes, containing fans, reduced the stratification of air within the atrium.[77]

Prominent examples were also published in professional journals as technical studies prior to construction to showcase underpinning research. These largely revolved around the use of atrium spaces to provide enhanced daylight, as artificial lighting was considered to be a major factor in energy consumption, and to mitigate its heat effects. Physical models were often constructed for tests, and computational analyses fed the design process. These cases included Caudill Rowlett Scott's (CRS) proposal for the offices for Shell Oil in Houston (1980),[78] a series of linked triangular atrium forms with shallow perimeter offices; CRS's collaborative effort with Van der Ryn/Calthorpe & Partners, The Architects' Collaborative, and the Tennessee Valley Authority's Architectural Design Branch on the latter's headquarters in Chattanooga (1984), which consisted of two linear buildings with full-length atriums, where, again, daylighting was the main technical determinant of the design;[79] a proposal for the Solar Energy Research Institute Headquarters in rural Golden, Colorado (1980), designed by the consortium Table Mountain Architects, which again included CRS and the prominent energy design consultancy Dubin-Bloome Associates, where a series of low, linear atriums or "solar courts" cascaded down a hillside, with the collection and storage of solar energy a centerpiece of the design;[80] and an urban-scaled speculative proposal based on research undertaken at the US National Bureau of Standards' Center for Building

Figure 3.7 State Office Building (Bateson Building), Sacramento, California. State Architect of California (Sim Van der Ryn and Peter Calthorpe), 1981. Courtesy Simon Sadler.

Technology, exploring the idea of "solar planning" for northeastern cities. The proposal involved creating canopies with south-facing glazing in a serrated roof profile along commercial streets to provide energy efficiency for adjacent buildings and to spur downtown revitalization efforts.[81] An overview of atrium design for energy conservation in North America was published in *Progressive Architecture* in 1982. It provided commentary on several prominent atrium buildings and attempted to shift the professional debate toward the energy-saving potentials of atriums.[82] Case studies of atrium buildings also started to feature in ASHRAE publications, including a study of a building proposed by the Energy Systems Research Laboratory at Oak Ridge, California, by architect Burford Duke,[83] and an analysis of John Andrews's Intelsat Headquarters in Washington (1984), where the building's HVAC system combined low-energy solutions with advanced fire safety measures across the building's five, linked atriums.[84]

Across these publications, a series of principles was beginning to emerge regarding how the atrium performed for environmental and energy efficiency. The stack effect featured prominently, whereby fresh air would be drawn through the depth of a building, allowing hot air to rise through an atrium and be expelled at the top. The atrium's role as a buffer zone or indeterminate inside/outside space was also emphasized. The benefits of natural lighting, especially in deep-plan buildings, were also acknowledged, as was the idea that the volume of air in an atrium could be used as a plenum to supply, extract, or recirculate air as an integral part of a building's HVAC system.[85]

Despite these kinds of publications and the levels of interest they garnered regarding the energy credentials of the atrium, a gap was beginning to emerge between the publication of exemplar buildings and the provision of research findings that could further inform the design and engineering professions. As one ASHRAE member noted, while atriums designed with energy efficiency in mind could be shown to deliver results, their success was largely based on "the design skills and experience of the project team."[86] By the mid-1990s, however, ASHRAE publications began to feature articles on recent research emerging from Europe and the United Kingdom. One reported on the International Energy Agency's (IEA) Task XI research project "Passive and Hybrid Solar Commercial Buildings," funded by the Norwegian Council for Scientific and Industrial Research. A strand focusing on atriums was led by Anne Grete Hestnes from the Norwegian Institute of Technology and was structured around analyses of sixteen European case studies—including Arup Associates' Gateway Two—the development of computer simulation tools for designers, and the provision of design guidance.[87] A similar program by the Energy Technology Support Unit (ETSU), initiated under the aegis of the UK Department of Environment, was also featured. The program pursued two kinds of research in order to provide guidance for architects and engineers: assessments of successful designs in the form of Energy Performance Assessments—including, again, an assessment of Gateway Two[88]—and studies that would "illustrate the design process in achieving a successful solution and examine alternative options, economic considerations, etc.—in fact, all the issues with which a designer would have to be concerned in practice in developing such a scheme."[89]

An ETSU publication that collected together four of these design studies was explicit about the utility of this mode of transferring knowledge to professional architects, the design study being "a more effective vehicle for spreading information than research reports."[90] Focusing on passive solar design and adopting a method employed by the American Institute of Architects in their Building Energy Performance Standards research project of 1977, the Energy Performance Assessment was a scheme that engaged the architects of an existing building to redesign it with energy saving as the main objective, while still adhering to the original conditions of the brief: site, program, level of specification, and cost.[91] The four cases published either involved the redesign of an existing atrium or the incorporation of a new one within the design. The existing and redesigned buildings were then subject to energy analysis by a team of specialist advisors. ETSU funded a range of studies and reports on energy-efficient buildings in which atriums featured heavily, including the report *Atrium Buildings: Numbers and Future Trends*,[92] which aimed to project future trends in energy-conscious atrium design to 2030, and Hawkes's *An Architect's Guide to the General Principles of Energy-Conscious Atrium Building Design*,[93] which gathered together all the relevant research on atriums, including the findings of the IEA project, and presented it in a manner that could be practically used by architects in designing atrium buildings.

The research of the Cambridge team would also continue along these lines, the atrium being integral to performance and analysis tools they developed, including Nick Baker and Koen Steemers's LT (Lighting and Thermal) Method, a calculation tool for nondomestic buildings that included specific parameters for atriums,[94] and their edited volume arising from an EU-funded initiative on daylighting which, again, made specific reference to atrium buildings.[95] Research projects of this kind would continue to flourish in the northern hemisphere through the 1990s, developing computational models for assessing the energy and environmental performance of atriums[96] and applying these kinds of methods to the analysis of built examples, often over several years.[97]

★★★

Across this trajectory of research and practice the atrium building might be seen as something of a salvation, a return, albeit via different means, to the architectural modulation of indoor climate. Indeed, many better-performing, healthier buildings featuring atriums have been designed and constructed.[98] However, the passive or at least multidimensional techniques of environmental control that the atrium promoted are not inherent in the form. Portman's model that Greenberg flipped could just as easily be flipped back. Research on the environmental performance of atrium buildings was thus predicated on continual verification. New tools and techniques developed for better performance needed testing; new built or projected examples needed analyses to assess their performance. Case studies provided the means for assessment, and guidance made best practice available to architects.

This situation might be compared to the rise of engineering-based research into the fire safety of atrium buildings. As we have seen in chapter 2, the dynamic behavior of a fire in an atrium, and the complex interaction between the techniques and technologies assembled to mitigate its impact, had to be tested or simulated via scenarios or models. Such scenario-based testing began to replace prescriptive regulations that were established to be absolute and broadly applied, and fire safety engineering was increasingly given a licensing role in this new, performance-based regulatory procedure.

Fire remains a rare event, and a shift to a performance-based approach to safety was understood within a framework that increasingly valued a professional willingness to take on risk. By contrast, energy consumption is inherent in buildings' daily use, and performance came to be understood as the active management of a dynamic and variable environment in this quotidian sense. Analyses of energy performance would not seem to belong to a realm of risk, except where individual buildings could fail significantly in terms of energy use, comfort, or health, as was the case with instances of sick building syndrome. And yet the demonstration of environmental performance has relied on scenarios and modeling in much the same way as that of safety performance has. Such energy analyses, even those involving user feedback, have produced performance models that depend on certain variables of the dynamic environment. These models have been made available via guidance for architects, who have used the parameters as design aids. As a material and spatial condition, rather than a technical device, the atrium has made the manipulation of these parameters a part of architectural design. In stimulating new ways of calculating thermal balance—and offering energy-saving advantages—the atrium pulled apart assumptions about how that balance could be achieved and showed that the variability of the indoor environment opened up various opportunities to achieve comfort. It gave space to the architect to design variable solutions, including parameters that could be adjusted by occupants, rather than to apply standard ones.

We might understand this situation as the architect triumphing over the HVAC engineer, or at least becoming the professional responsible for organizing the variables of the indoor environment. Yet, much in the same way that the absence of certain statutory articles of fire codes for atriums exposed architects to risks inherent in their design decisions, architects also faced risks, and associated liabilities, that accumulated around the integration of variable components in a complex environmental system.

The designed management of variability, if not instability, became a sign of professional competence, of the architect's ability to take control of a design process and to produce innovative and often striking spatial solutions. New kinds of designs could be proposed to solve the problems older ones presented. Demonstrating this capability was part of the business climate architecture would embrace in the wake of deregulation.

In this way the modeling of a building's environmental performance became "performative." An energy-sensitive atrium design had a particular rhetorical function to garner agreement, rather than necessarily to lower energy consumption or maintain a healthy indoor environment, as demonstrable outcomes of this kind were often deferred.[99] Immediately after the energy crisis and at the point when sick building syndrome emerged, the environmentally performing—and performative—atrium became a hedge against the risks that indoor environments were increasingly posing.

4

Organizing

"We are all now on the wrong side of the office boom, consolidating at the bottom of the market as the optimists say."[1] Such a pronouncement by the editors of a manual on office planning published in the United States and the United Kingdom in 1976 might have constituted the last words of its epilogue, a wry admission about an untimely publishing project. It was in fact the first line of the introduction, "consolidation" code for a complete rethink of the way office buildings could be conceived, designed, and constructed. *Planning Office Space*, edited by Francis Duffy, Colin Cave, and John Worthington, was a handbook for architects and their clients and provided a shared store of information and techniques to aid in joint decision making in the procurement, delivery, and management of office space. Aside from chapters on practicalities including planning, economics, regulation, servicing, environmental control, and management in use, the handbook's key idea was that the office could be described in terms of layers: shell, scenery, and sets. The shell was the building itself; the scenery, as in a theater, was the assembled elements required inside the shell for a particular tenant; and sets were the distribution of these elements according to the range of a tenant's needs. These layers had different life expectancies. A shell should be expected to last decades, scenery for several years, and sets for a shorter time, perhaps a few months. These described different degrees of change within the context of a speculative office market. Buildings were durable, but not eternal. Tenancies were assumed to be leasehold, and tenants' requirements would change within their lease period.

Duffy and Worthington were principals and Cave an associate of a London-based design and planning consultancy established in 1971 that came to be known as DEGW. Their efforts toward consolidation paid off, as by the mid-1980s the London office market was booming, taking advantage of a business and regulatory environment that had entirely changed because of the pro-free-market policies of Margaret Thatcher's Conservative government. As Amy Thomas has shown, the large-scale selloff of public assets and the financial "big bang" her government unleashed created the need for new, and new kinds of, office space, with corporations emerging in industries that had recently become competitive, including telecommunications, media, and financial services. In turn, developer-led models of urban transformation were prioritized through regulatory overhaul, allowing for the large-scale provision of office space to drive transformation largely freed from former planning restrictions. As a space-planning and organizational consultancy, rather than simply an architectural firm, DEGW positioned itself to manage the risks inherent in this new, entrepreneurial environment of office development. It provided specialist, knowledge-based services that understood organizational needs and the changes that technology would bring to corporations and the work taking place within them. Indeed, by the early 1980s, the requirement for computerization in office work had become as important as structure, scenery, and sets.[2]

Emblematic of this new approach to office development was 1 Finsbury Avenue, an atrium building completed in 1984 by Arup Associates, with principal architect Peter Foggo, for Stuart Lipton's development company Rosehaugh Greycoat Estates. It was situated next to what would later become the Broadgate development, adjacent to Liverpool Street Station and just outside the historic boundary of the City of London, the capital's

Figure 4.1 1 Finsbury Avenue, London. Arup Associates, 1984. Heritage Image Partnership Ltd / Alamy.

Figure 4.2 1 Finsbury Avenue, London. Arup Associates, 1984. Initial configuration of atrium. Drawing by Sophie Lanigan and Oskar Johanson.

Figure 4.3 1 Finsbury Avenue, London. Arup Associates, 1984. Renovated atrium, 1998. Drawing by Sophie Lanigan and Oskar Johanson.

financial center.[3] While not directly involved with the design of 1 Finsbury Avenue, DEGW had consulted on the brief and space planning and had designed the interiors for Arup Associates' Gateway Two in Basingstoke (1983), a building which featured a full-height, naturally ventilated atrium. 1 Finsbury Avenue was clearly a development of the formal concept of Gateway Two. Fully air-conditioned, 1 Finsbury Avenue contained an atrium that ran through its eight floors, capped at the top by an octagonal glazed dome. Where Gateway Two was a commission from a single company, 1 Finsbury Avenue was designed as a speculative office building, Arup Associates' first venture into that market, with 300,000 square feet of lettable floor space.[4]

The design for 1 Finsbury Avenue was a novel response to the problem of the deep-plan building. One commentator remarked that the atrium made it possible "to have the developer's magic number window-to-window dimension of 45 feet"[5]—the windows to the atrium were understood to be "exterior"—while maintaining deep dimensions across the whole building, maximizing site coverage. The building's overall lighting and HVAC requirements were equivalent to those of a slab building, and the atrium offered energy benefits by mitigating heat loss through the atrium facades. Two cores on the north and south sides of the atrium, with adjacent escape stairs at the building's west and east edges, meant that the floorplates could effectively be divided into four separate quadrants on each floor or combined together for half- or whole-floor occupation, giving flexibility for leasing.[6] The latter potential, an advantage of the deep building, won out, as firms such as stockbrokers Rowe & Pittman leased entire floors, joining together the parts of their operation that had been housed in separate buildings.[7]

The building's flexibility was illustrated when, just one year after completion, four floors were upgraded for investment bank SG Warburg, which had acquired Rowe & Pittman, in readiness for the financial "big bang." This involved fitting 200 miles of cabling below the building's raised floors, whose depth had to be increased, to service new electronic trading terminals. The HVAC system also needed boosting to cope with the extra heat generated by the computer equipment.[8] By 1996, through an amalgamation with the Swiss Banking Corporation, the new entity SBC Warburg had become the building's sole tenant, as well as that of the development's phase two building, 2 Finsbury Avenue. In a retrofit completed by Arup Associates in 1998 the atrium was bridged over at the third-floor level to provide one continuous trading floor across the entirety of the floorplate, with the floor below housing the IT equipment to service it. The two further dealer floors above the new trading level were opened to the atrium to create the feeling of one connected space. The raised floors became three times deeper, reversing the design of the HVAC system, with air delivered from below, effectively cooling the computer equipment, though the cooling load doubled and backup power generation was increased. A new glazed ceiling was installed below the atrium dome to filter light for the trading floor. The occupation of an atrium that had once had no designated function was enabled by a new fire safety design, with an Arup-engineered system accommodating innovative fire sprinklers, smoke detection, and venting.[9]

The design of 1 Finsbury Avenue has been seen as deeply influenced by the findings of one of DEGW's most significant industry reports, the ORBIT Study, which was released in 1983. The report outlined the future impact of information technology on office work and office buildings. One of its key findings was that rapid changes in computing and telecommunications would make users more dependent on buildings, not less, and that flexibility had to be built into future office building design to address this.[10] It resituated the approaches described in *Planning Office Space*, in particular the relationships between shell, scenery, and sets, and outlined the role the architect—or the space planning consultant—could take in a context where private enterprise would drive the development of office buildings and the kinds of work within them.[11] As Thomas has argued, DEGW "reimagined the processes and professional relationships that underpinned the production of commercial architecture."[12]

We might also see 1 Finsbury Avenue as the instantiation of Dean Hawkes and Richard MacCormac's model office design of 1978, for which Duffy consulted on the office layout. While that design was presented primarily in terms of its energy efficiency, something which would be rendered moot by the enormous power and cooling needs of successive waves of computing installations at 1 Finsbury Avenue, Hawkes and MacCormac's reflection on their design framed a larger argument about what was at stake in the transformations described by Duffy and DEGW. Hawkes and MacCormac were attempting to juggle a legacy of office design that was often presented in two divergent possibilities: the cellular and the open plan, two forms of planning that had become ascendant in the United States by midcentury.[13] They also dealt with the aftermath of Bürolandschaft, an office design movement that had sought to tackle this dichotomy. An invention of German management consultants, Bürolandschaft sought to diagram a new relationship between work, employee, and corporate organization, one that was built on understanding and enhancing communication between employees within a democratic and deliberative corporate culture. It promoted the dynamic arrangement of clusters of moveable furniture distributed across an unencumbered deep floorplate. Hawkes and MacCormac didn't hew to this technique, but their design amplified, in a different way, the social interaction so prized in the Bürolandschaft theory. In their design, a ground-level mall would link the atriums together to "generate some of the characteristics of an urban street relating to shared amenities such as restaurants and shops or creches."[14]

In the mid-1960s, Duffy had been Bürolandschaft's key advocate in the English-speaking world, publishing the primer *Office Landscaping: A New Approach to Office Planning* in 1966. By the time *Planning Office Space* appeared a decade later, he would repudiate what had become, by then, a much-criticized form of office organization, even though he drew many lessons from it. What had emerged in the gap between Duffy's two publications was the atrium, and several of his key writings on architecture through the 1980s and '90s were reviews of prominent atrium buildings.

While they didn't remark upon Bürolandschaft, these reviews carried its lessons through into a professional and economic reality that increasingly focused on the employee as a particular kind of subject, one inexorably shaped by and responsive to the vectors of change that office organization materialized. These changes included the kind of rapid spatial and technical renovations seen at 1 Finsbury Avenue, as well as the potentials of social interaction presaged by Hawkes and MacCormac in their streetlike mall. Indeed, these kinds of changes went hand in hand and were registered not only in a building's spatiality and materiality, but in employees' comportment to them as they became the subject of—and subject to—the changing workplace of corporate identity and change management.

★★★

Duffy presented Bürolandschaft to the English-speaking world in a 1964 article in the *Architectural Review*, and this led to a commission for a monograph two years later.[15] He had been on a trip to Germany to visit current examples and to meet Wolfgang and Eberhard Schnelle,[16] the organizational consultants and publishers who, together with their multidisciplinary group known as the Quickborner Team, had invented Bürolandschaft. As Andreas Rumpfhuber has written, their office planning method drew on the team's development, from the mid-1950s, of a "cybernetics of organization, which aspired to free all workers from tedious work through full automation, and ultimately to dismiss workers into the everlasting spare time of the social-liberal welfare state."[17] It drew on philosophical and theoretical backings that saw society as a complex organization of differentiated and often oppositional parts, yet one that was held together by the communication between them. This formulation became a central tenet of Bürolandschaft: "its design is pragmatically geared toward and incorporates dissenting opinions as knowledge feedback within the organization."[18] These opinions were those of the knowledge worker, a subject relatively freed from the repetitive banalities of routine office work and able to exercise judgment and informed decision making.[19] As Rumpfhuber has argued, their feedback and "opinion" would be characterized as a responsibility to the organization in achieving its goals. To process and therefore shape such a responsibility, the procedures of these employees' work would need to become clearly understood and articulated as a function of communication.[20]

The Quickborner team studied and analyzed these procedures by charting how communication happened within an organization. The members of the team would document the type, movement, and frequency of communications, from paperwork moving within and between different departments to phone calls and informal communications between workers. Their research enabled work processes in an office to be formalized and optimized, and it would directly inform how an office landscape would be equipped and laid out.[21]

The Quickborner team would translate the quantitative information gained from their studies into scaled drawings of an organization's different departments. These departments would be linked together with lines of different thickness that represented the frequency of communication between them. Their relationship to each other would then be arranged according to these lines, with more frequent communication meaning closer proximity. The same technique would be worked through within each department, with workers and their functions, and the equipment they needed such as desks and filing cabinets, represented by scaled cutouts that could then be arrayed to form organizational plans.[22]

A Bürolandschaft layout had a particular spatial character. Tightly packed floes of office equipment—desks, chairs, meeting tables, cupboards, filing systems—organized according to their internal communication dynamic would be distributed on a large, open office floor. Their irregular edges would be defined by various forms of screening, including moveable dividers and planters to aid privacy. These in turn would indicate the passages of movement through the office floor and demarcate the entry arrangements of each individual area. Along with the usual servicing an

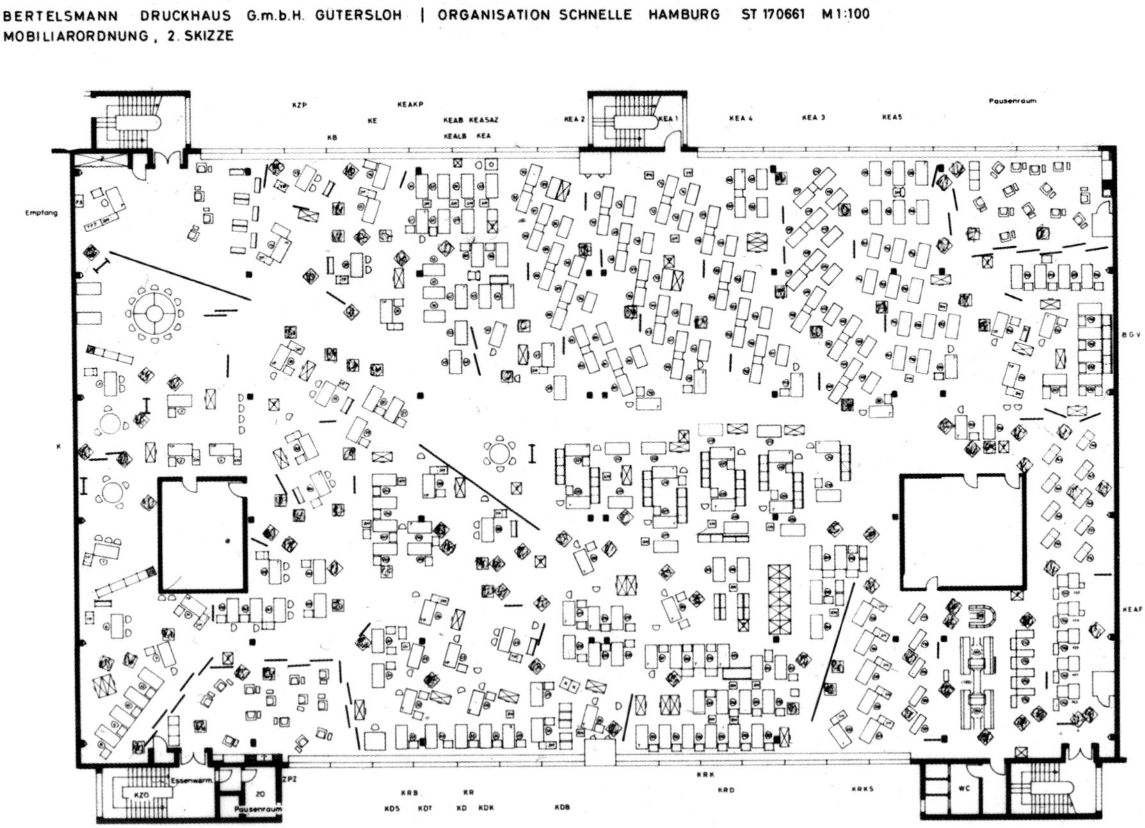

Figure 4.4 Office layout for Buch und Ton / Bertelsmann, Gütersloh, Germany. Quickborner Team, 1961. Quickborner Archive. Courtesy Andreas Rumpfhuber.

office required, generous common rest areas would be provided to allow for the informal communications and casual breaks prized within the Quickborner theory of communication.

While the Bürolandschaft arrangement seemed disorderly at first sight—especially, as Duffy noticed, in photographs[23]—it was governed by a series of rules to ensure the correct application of the patterns developed for each part of the organization. These included orientations to provide coherence for a department and preserve worker privacy, basic sizing and distance standards, ease of movement within areas and between them, and arrangement of meeting spaces to preserve acoustic privacy.[24] Particular architectural and environmental aspects underpinned this arrangement. Bürolandschaft relied on the deep-plan building, which necessitated air-conditioning and an even distribution of artificial lighting. Ceiling heights needed to be low to aid the acoustic performance of the office space. Carpeting was also specified to soften noise as well as to introduce what Duffy characterized as a domestic way of inhabiting the space.[25]

Rumpfhuber has argued that, even in Bürolandschaft's potential for spatial and material adaptability, the Quickborner team saw that office space itself was "soon to be obsolete." The real object of their research was the organization and management of work itself, underpinned by the cybernetic idea that control would "no longer [happen] through the hardware of architecture but through the software of social relations, through the calculated flow of information within the organization."[26] The preface to Quickborner team member Alfons Wankum's *Layout Planning in the Landscaped Office* was blunter: "In actual fact, office landscaping is a total planning approach in which the cybernetics of information processing are fundamental. Together with the longer-range plans of the occupier, they determine the space in which a controlled environment will be created. It is only at this point that the layout planner appears on the scene."[27]

Within a research-based, cybernetic understanding of the optimization and management of work, the physical organization of an office was a tool, rather than an endpoint. In a way reminiscent of—and concomitant with—the setup that structured research into HVAC systems and indoor environmental comfort, the Schnelle brothers' requirements constituted the controlled conditions approaching those of a lab: an unencumbered, deep floorplate with an even, artificial environment to allow for experimentation with layout and to enable further comparative organizational research. As Eberhard Schnelle remarked: "The discovery of similar patterns or structures in many concrete tasks puts the organizer in a position to compare socio-technical systems and to develop methods of improving the performance of these systems."[28] Indeed, for the Quickborner team and their publishing arm Verlag Schnelle, the overarching goal was to provide knowledge regarding cybernetics and its application to organizational problems.[29]

For Duffy, however, the application was direct and architectural. He situated Bürolandschaft squarely within the evolution of office planning, and in relation to what he considered to be the divergence of choice between cellular and open-plan layouts. These layouts emerged in relation to various architectural and commercial constraints, including structure, plan depth, servicing, and environmental systems, as well as urban development and regulation. For Duffy, Bürolandschaft represented "not a gimmick but a real advance," a "middle way" between the two modes of layout.[30] His guide to the technique was free of philosophical or systems thinking except as it informed the practical method employed to develop an office organization that both employer and employee would be seen to benefit from.[31]

By the mid-1970s, however, Duffy's enthusiasm for Bürolandschaft had diminished, in large part because the surface application of Bürolandschaft techniques had produced packed, messy, open plan spaces with none of the finesse of the original versions. The European enthusiasm for them had also soured, employees' "dissenting opinions" being manifest through workers' councils that gave them a legislated voice in the processes of organizational governance, including the design of office space.[32] By this time Duffy had developed his own theoretical approach to the problem of office planning through formal study with Christopher Alexander at the University of California, Berkeley, and then at Princeton University with sociologist

Robert Guttman. The PhD dissertation Duffy submitted at Princeton in 1974 sought to test correspondences between organizational structure and office layout.[33] In large part it was a critique of Bürolandschaft.

Planning Office Space followed quickly and constituted his, and DEGW's, own method and manual for office organization. It also presented the critique of Bürolandschaft, with two essays that characterized it as a problematic, short-lived experiment. One essay by architect and sociologist Bevis Fuller provided a theoretical refutation of the central tenets of Bürolandschaft theory and method.[34] The main charge was of environmental determinism, the misconception that enhanced communication between workers would flow from a layout designed for that enhancement. Fuller argued that sociological understanding of interpersonal relationships, rather than a communications-based theory of social relations, would yield a far more complex picture of what motivated or demotivated individuals in their work. Fuller's academic critique opened the way for Duffy's own reconsideration, written with Colin Cave, of the method of which he had been an ardent supporter a decade earlier. Duffy and Cave cast Bürolandschaft as a grab bag of mismatched ideologies: "Latter day Taylorism vies with updated human relations; human relations thinking conflicts with environmental determinism. Perhaps the only common factor of these ideas is that they are slightly out of date."[35]

Notwithstanding this critique, much of what underpinned Bürolandschaft remained in place in Duffy's own method, even as—or especially since—it was framed in the pragmatic terms of the real estate market in the United Kingdom, where, unlike those in Continental Europe, corporations would be unlikely to procure and own their office buildings. Multidisciplinary teams would remain important: "architects working with managers, office managers working with interior designers; developers with market researchers, space planners with cost accountants."[36] User studies, primarily framed in terms of user needs and satisfaction, would be emphasized, but were certainly not the sole determinant of organizational knowledge. Other stakeholders, including developers of speculative office buildings, were seen to be just as important. Methods were valued that would attempt to gain a holistic understanding of an organization and its needs, articulated as part of a "program" rather than a definitive brief.[37] There should be a relationship between the management structure of an organization and the physical layout of its offices, though in a way that avoided what the authors termed the "distinct moral edge" of Bürolandschaft's supposedly democratic management style and the physical openness of its spatial correlate.[38] An approach to flexibility as appropriate to an organization's need was valued within a particular layout but more importantly in relation to what would be undefined future organizational needs. Proper servicing of office space and an awareness of the office as an environment remained important, as did an openness to technological change, framed by Bürolandschaft as automation but more broadly understood by Duffy in terms of the changing nature of work.

Most importantly, Duffy and Cave salvaged from Bürolandschaft the impetus for DEGW's own consultancy model: "office landscaping seemed the closest approximation to a service which it was felt architects and interior designers were failing to supply—the detailed planning of interior space by people who understood something both of design and organisational structure."[39] This possibility meant Duffy could be expansive: "Office design is prototypical of the future of a great part of all building design. What makes it potentially so rich an example is the close relationship between the workplace and the worker and between the whole stock of space and the user organisation. Feedback from the users in these circumstances ought to be very powerful." And finally, Duffy thought that "we can probably expect a blurring of the boundaries between office space and other building types such as factories, shops, health centres."[40]

★★★

It was this sense of blurring between offices and other building types that captured something hitherto unarticulated in Duffy's embrace—and subsequent critique—of Bürolandschaft. It offered the possibility of enlarging what had been the intraoffice communicational dynamic that was central to Bürolandschaft. Communication within an organization could now be characterized in terms of the proximity to different amenities and functions. A further decade after *Planning Office Space* Duffy's model for this was to be found in Scandinavia, in Niels Torp's headquarters for the airline SAS in a landscaped site on the edge of Stockholm (1987). The building consisted of a series of cranked, linear office blocks fronting a glazed street that created an urban amenity of the kind Hawkes and MacCormac had imagined in their model office design. The urban, communicational realm of the street was generous. Punctuated by neat rows of *Ficus benjamina*, the enclosed, atrium-like street descended to the north of the site via two sets of stairs, which were combined with gentle waterfalls to overlook a landscaped lake. A round gathering place marked the street's midpoint, and the building blocks abutting the street were joined across its width by banks of glazed bridges. Exposed stairs and elevator shafts punctuated the street, and variously sized terraces and balconies projected from the buildings to overlook it at different levels. Opening onto the street were the social amenities that were so prominent in the brief: sports hall, gym, swimming pool and sauna, health center, bank and travel agency, grocery store, clothes boutique, library, a café and dining rooms, as well as conference center and auditorium. Concerts and performances often occurred on the street at lunchtimes and in the evening.[41]

The five low-rise office blocks that fronted onto the street each housed a different department within the airline's structure, and their floorplates were divided between cellular offices—almost all the 1,500 employees were provided one—and a common space, or "multiroom," that sat at the center of a branch of around 20 offices. The multiroom was, in part, a Swedish version of Bürolandschaft's common rest area, though the arrangement of cellular and shared space owed nothing to the German planning method. Indeed, the multiroom can be seen to have actively refuted it in allowing the individual worker their own space for autonomous work, and the

Figure 4.5 SAS Headquarters, Stockholm. Niels Torp + Architects, 1987. Nordic Photos / Superstock.

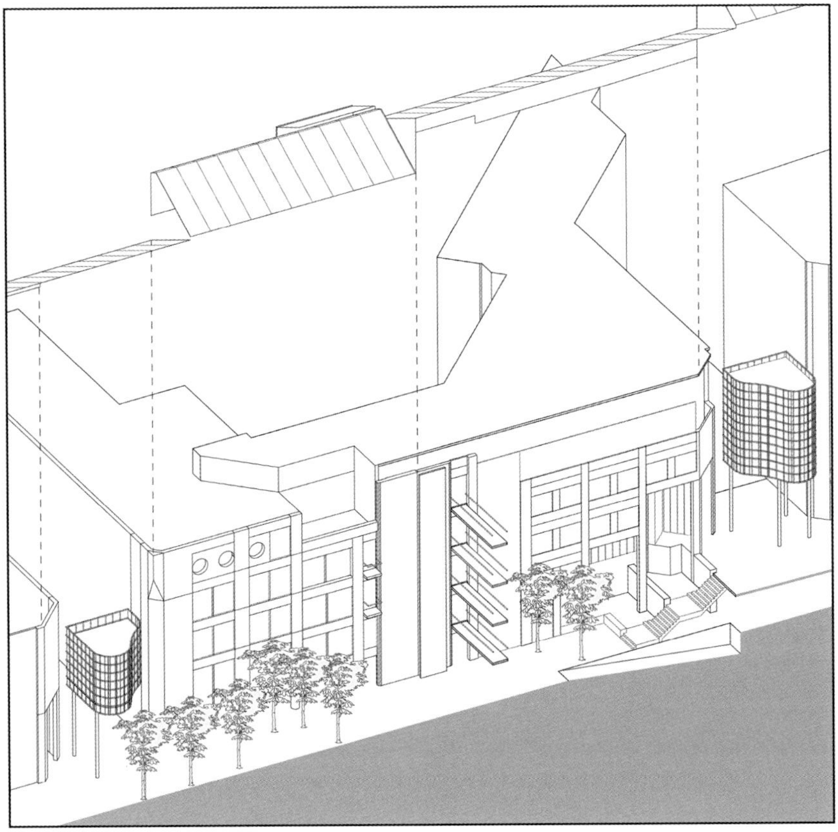

Figure 4.6 SAS Headquarters, Stockholm. Niels Torp + Architects, 1987. Drawing by Sophie Lanigan and Oskar Johanson.

opportunity to join with colleagues to engage as a group. This diagram of individual and common space on each office floor underpinned the building's larger arrangement of separate departments and the common street.

Duffy's critique of the SAS Headquarters, published in the *Architectural Review*, saw this multifunctional communicational arrangement as a direct result of the vision of the SAS chief executive, Jan Carlzon. Carlzon was reported as saying: "The main task for the administration would be to provide service for the front line, and to develop and formulate visions, strategies and goals. We wanted to put all this in the architecture."[42] Duffy adumbrated the spatial characteristics of this ideology of management: it "is an architecture of serendipity, of interconnections, of networking; an architecture within which people can meet spontaneously; where crossing departmental boundaries is easy; where everyone is close by."[43] He contrasted this with hierarchical value systems, made manifest in the very materiality of "chairs, desks, partitions, lighting, ceiling grids, the curtain walls" that perpetuated "an imagery of power and control derived from corporate life as it existed at the beginning of the [twentieth] century."[44]

In its bespoke response to a managerialism of "visions, strategies and goals," Duffy characterized the building as breaking "every rule of Anglo-Saxon property development."[45] It privileged user input and user experience, balancing this between individual autonomy (the private office) and group participation (the multiroom; the street). Where the Anglo-Saxon "system" demanded flexibility in relation to the market and the future needs of corporations, Sweden's "long social democratic tradition" could afford, literally, through its "higher GDP per capita" to position the individual within the corporation in such a bespoke way.[46] While Duffy would finally judge that the building would not be flexible enough to adapt to the sorts of changes that were being brought about by information technology, together with what he saw as the inevitability of corporate change and further evolutions of work culture, a lesson was evident in what he saw as the building's "knowing and commercial use of architectural resources."[47] In its social-democratic context, that commerciality was just as much a reality as 1 Finsbury Avenue's market-based speculation. SAS's atrium-cum-street was just as "flexible" in providing for, and managing, the desired relationship between individual and corporation. Chairs, desks, partitions, lighting, ceiling grids, and curtain walls may well have materialized a certain ideology of the office and of work, but cafés, waterfalls, gyms, multirooms, and *Ficus benjamina* did as well.

Duffy concluded his critique of the SAS Headquarters with the following thoughts: "it is inevitable that we will have to design to these standards in Britain before very long," and that "[t]here are too many provocative and stimulating lessons to be learned from the building as an instrument of advanced, late twentieth century corporate policy."[48]

An approach to architecture that expanded the communicational domain of the office in this fashion did land in the United Kingdom in the early 1990s in the form of a speculative office building called The Ark (1992), designed by Swedish-based UK émigré Ralph Erskine, and it caught Duffy's attention.[49] Placed in a difficult site between a railway line and a freeway flyover in West London, the ovoid building bulged outward like the hull of a great ship or, as Martin Pawley put it, "half barge, half spaceship, half Ewok tree house."[50] Brick-faced buttresses and columns rose through the bonze-colored, canted glass and metal facade, and emerged as towers and turrets above a roof line that sloped to the south. Inside, through a low entranceway containing a café-pub, the atrium emerged as a dramatic vista. It was less the elegant, convivial street of the SAS Headquarters, more a turreted medieval town center, albeit one abstracted in a typical Scandinavian palette of white walls and blond wood, accentuated by Erskine's textural brick detailing. Bridges cut across the atrium, while cascading terraces and balconies established vantages to look down into and through it. A belvedere atop a tower commanded the central focus, while gondola elevators rose through the space. The atrium reproduced the variegated profile and formal play the building itself presented on the skyline.

Surrounding this visual excitement were remarkably conventional open floorplates that could be configured as in any London speculative

Figure 4.7 The Ark, London. Ralph Erskine, 1992. Peter Cook / VIEW.

development. These rose to eight floors on the north and five on the south. Despite the outwardly slanting exterior walls and curve-laden plan, Duffy was surprised that a consistent grid and allowances for acoustic separation made the plan extremely adaptable, though all levels were open to the atrium. An innovative HVAC system that included radiant cooling panels in the ceiling and air extraction at the bottom of the atrium combined Swedish norms with advanced technology. As with 1 Finsbury Avenue's 1990s refurbishment, the atrium's openness was made possible by advancements in fire technology overseen by Margaret Law at Arup, including a long-throw sprinkler system and the use of the upper level of the atrium as a smoke-logging plenum.[51]

As with Torp, Erskine was keen to promote a culture of openness and collaboration through his design. As he surmised, "eight or nine interacting intellectual companies can work here." Workers would meet in the café-pub "at the base of the atrium in a social space that will be like a small medieval town. Here they will talk about their different businesses and find they have things in common and somehow develop new ways of working."[52]

The building was originally planned to be the London headquarters of its Swedish developer Åke Larson who would have hand-picked the other tenants to occupy the building.[53] However the UK arm of the developer went into receivership due to the recession of the early 1990s—Sweden also experienced its own financial crisis at this time—and it was forced to sell the building. Despite its vaunted potential, the building stood empty for four years. A plan by the new owners to install escalators to make it more amenable to multitenancy was not implemented,[54] and in 1996 it became the London headquarters of Seagram, the corporation interested in the work culture the building could facilitate, using the consolidation of business units previously housed in different buildings as part of a corporate change strategy.[55] They departed in 2000, however, as the result of a takeover, which again left the building vacant. In 2006 the building was sold by its German owners as a consequence of the German recession of that year. The new owner, a UK real estate investment firm, proposed to "de-quirk the internal workings of the building and create more regular, functional floorplates that are in line with the requirements of mainstream corporate occupiers."[56] This involved removing the village of informal meeting spaces and filling in parts of the atrium space to increase the size of the floorplates, which were then glazed on their atrium side. The atrium itself was divided into two smaller ones, effectively turning "a doughnut plan into a pretzel."[57]

Despite the perturbations of the market, the lesson of The Ark was not one of failure. While Duffy might have thought that an atrium of this kind would bring the experience of Scandinavian work culture to London—in its initial form he thought that it provided "an ideal setting for the inevitable increase in the public life of the office"[58]—the atrium showed a promise entirely consistent with 1 Finsbury Avenue and the SAS Headquarters, being adaptable to any ideology that came its way, including the various versions of lettable office space.

★★★

Yet The Ark did lack something that went hand in hand with the spatial potential seen in the SAS Headquarters: the active management of human relations. The building's complete exposure to the market highlighted the value of management's mediating function. As Duffy's consultancy model for DEGW demonstrated, management was not something that remained solely with the client after the building was completed. Rather, it was constituted in the interaction between the client and the architect from the very beginning of the briefing process, and its presence would be felt long after a building was completed. When the Scandinavian model again came to London, Duffy would enact DEGW's management function to process the relationship between employee and office organization.

DEGW consulted on the briefing of Niels Torp's new headquarters for British Airways (BA), known as Waterside, which was completed in 1998 on a landscaped site at the edge of Heathrow Airport in London. Duffy

Figure 4.8 BA Waterside, London. Niels Torp + Architects, 1998. Janet Hall / RIBA Collections.

again gave a critique of the building and combined it with a more academic reflection that evaluated the trajectory of DEGW's planning method in a context where the atrium had become a prominent spatial technique.

Waterside's architectural diagram and functional amenity were, for all intents and purposes, a copy of the SAS Headquarters. The building consisted of six U-shaped blocks that fronted a glazed street. Duffy was clear about the strategic relationship between the airline's management structure and the organizational diagram of the building. There was an explicit acknowledgment of the risk management strategy built into Waterside's fabric. Each of the so-called "houses" that fronted the street could be divided or divested in the event of the corporation's "demise."[59] This sense of adaptation was built into the diagram, rather than having to be the subject of a redesign as with The Ark or 1 Finsbury Avenue. The market problem, however, was not one of lettability but of corporate change in the aftermath of deregulation, BA having been fully privatized in 1987. As Duffy remarked: "Waterside is an example of a volatile organisation struggling to accommodate change within a long-term structure. Like many organisations, BA is deliberately using architecture to achieve business objectives."[60]

While Duffy placed the SAS Headquarters in the context of an inclusive, social-democratic culture of communication, of "serendipity" and "interconnections," his account of Waterside was more pragmatic: "the working environment has been deliberately and consistently deployed as part of an overall program of change management. The resource of office space has been co-ordinated with changes in information technology and human resources to affect every aspect of BA's culture."[61] At the SAS Headquarters, a distinct managerial method had been framed as innate cultural characteristic. At Waterside, the "strategic importance of how office design can transmit messages about business interaction has become overt."[62]

Duffy was at pains to describe a consultancy process that was inclusive of BA staff in the briefing for the building by means of "interviews, surveys and focus groups."[63] These culminated in staff needing to complete training modules in order to set foot in the building and begin working.[64] Employees were now explicitly framed as knowledge workers, the process of their consultation calling upon them to identify themselves as such.

In the end, Duffy thought that BA hadn't quite gone far enough. The Scandinavian model that Waterside copied still held a "static" relationship between individual employee and collaborative work, a relationship "which does not seem quite right for what is already a more temporary, more plural, more project based, more open-ended organisation."[65] He also thought that the building itself remained too hermetic and internally focused, whereas "barriers are likely to dissolve between big organisations like BA and their diverse and complex network of increasingly out-sourced advisors, specialists and suppliers."[66]

Reviewing the procurement of Waterside in the context of a deregulated, managerialized business environment, Duffy would ultimately stake a claim for the role of architectural research. Clarity of corporate objectives, combined with a thorough consultation, briefing, and design process, "should allow the difference between the previous state and today to be measured in a hundred ways."[67] This research-based approach can be thought of cybernetically, looping back to Bürolandschaft: inputs in the design phase would lead to outputs feeding back into an enhanced procedure. For both Duffy and the Quickborner team, research meant the production of knowledge about user needs and interaction, though the Quickborner team's contribution was firmly lodged at the level of management research. In this light, Duffy's building critiques can be seen as a form of knowledge transfer, articulting organizational problems and ways to frame and solve them architecturally. As such they were bespoke communications of his and DEGW's expertise.

★★★

The specific lessons of the atrium were not the subject of extended reflection or theorization in Duffy's critiques. Yet, in the wake of Bürolandschaft, the atrium was able to adapt to changing theories and practices regarding the relationship between users and buildings, as well as to accommodate the physical changes that attended these. It could perform this way because of its "additional" status, as both an excess and a void at the core of an office building, rather than being designed as one element of office organization. The atrium allowed for—and enticed—activities and forms of engagement that took place away from the conventional office, desk, or workstation. It offered a (literal) view past the supposedly immediate concerns of work toward a larger horizon, or across into a realm of the organization that offered a reflection of an employee's own position. It also invited a certain kind of "informal" interaction where these enlarged perspectives might be recognized and shared. An atrium-sized trading room, as at 1 Finsbury Avenue, was not just an example of the physical adaptive capacity of the space. It was a manifestation of the organization's corporate culture. Similarly, the enclosed streets of the SAS Headquarters or Waterside allowed perspectives that took employees "outside" their regular work areas to demonstrate and reinforce, via a type of social interaction, the larger corporate structure in which they were enclosed.

Rather than accepting the critique that these kinds of buildings were cut off from their exterior contexts, we might consider that a large-scale incorporation was at stake. Employees would physically enter the world of the office, but that world was not separated, socially or materially, from their everyday life "outside." As a designed spatial intervention, the atrium as interior street was an intensification of the everyday, a heightened social condition that was itself the workplace. This mapped onto the atrium's variable, oscillating topology of outside-inside-outside, rendering a simple interior-exterior distinction outmoded.[68]

The atrium did not so much emphasize enclosure as amplify its effects to the level of a total environment, a condition without definite boundaries.[69] In doing so it went far beyond the "sites of confinement"—home, school, factory, prison—that Gilles Deleuze, following Michel Foucault, characterized as the topoi of modern, disciplinary societies and the model of productive labor they entailed.[70] The socially lubricated cognitive work of trading and of formulating corporate "visions, strategies and goals" was made, through the atrium, both highly visible and yet evanescent.

Where at 1 Finsbury Avenue the equipping of a vast trading room was initially framed as a problem of hardware and servicing, a demonstration of the incorporation of information technology Duffy had so keenly advocated, at the SAS Headquarters and at Waterside information was encoded and communicated as and within subjectivity itself. The trading floor was replaced by, and replicated within, the street of social interaction. In this sense the atrium was not a confining mold but what Deleuze called a form of modulation, a variable distribution enacting a form of control where one had the "freedom" to work in various self-motivated ways. What took place in the atrium was not productive work but the production of subjectivity as a kind of performance of the intellect.[71]

This was made most explicit in the moment that BA employees had to pass into the building via the calibrating grid of an induction program, an appraisal of knowledge regarding the building-cum-corporation and a mirror of the consultative process that entrained these employees in the first place. Success would bestow an individually encoded "passport," a license for the continual information trading of social-interaction-as-work. Whether or not the SAS Headquarters or Waterside could physically adjust to the future technical requirements of information technology was a moot point. Their model of information processing was already a "social" one, setting the scene for the coming-into-being of the material space of what Foucault called *homo economicus*, the "entrepreneur of himself,"[72] the subject negotiating the variabilities of the changing workplace and change management. As Deleuze wrote, in 1990, of the contemporary corporation: "businesses are constantly introducing an inexorable rivalry presented as healthy competition, a wonderful motivation that sets individuals against one another and sets itself up in each of them, dividing each within himself."[73]

The atrium marks a particular spatial threshold in corporate architecture, a designed material intervention that promoted the core of corporate work as a certain kind of self-managed "freedom." The atrium was a distinct strategy in the active management and control of social relations, the kind of "environmental" management entailed by, and entangled within, neoliberal governmentality.[74] In this context, *homo economicus* attained its definition for Foucault as the person "who responds systematically to modifications in the variables of the environment [and] appears precisely as someone manageable. . . . *Homo economicus* now becomes the correlate of a governmentality which will act on the environment and systematically modify its variables."[75] User research, feedback, continual consultancy, and managed intervention: DEGW's practice put to work a set of professional strategies and techniques that acted on the environment of the workplace, and these professional possibilities were themselves enabled by policies and techniques of deregulation that went to work on the professional environment of architecture itself.

5

Cultivating

> "Interiorscaping" is thus the new catchword. It comes from America and has been known here [in Europe] too for some two years. What is meant is the designing of large halls with plants. Using more or less ingenious measures, an impression of jungle, a touch of the South Seas with palm beach and sunset are imparted. The mixtures of plants are colourful and varied, the choice of species accidental to wrong, the spatial situation remains unmastered.[1]

In its potential to be a landscaped environment, the atrium enabled architecture to incorporate what had generally remained on the other side of the building envelope. Somewhat amused by the kitschness and ineptitude he was seeing in these efforts, German landscape architect Dieter Kienast was here prefacing a description of his own interior landscape project in the atrium of the Phonak AG Headquarters in Stäfa, Switzerland (1989), one that employed stands of bamboo to introduce what he thought of as a sense of tranquility and scale to an arcade-like atrium that ran the length of the three-story structure. Even with his landscape expertise, maintaining indoor plants was a complex undertaking, and Kienast pointed to problems

Figure 5.1 Phonak AG Headquarters, Stäfa, Switzerland. Burckhardt + Partner, 1989. © Archiv Burckhardt + Partner.

such as insect infestation and shedding of foliage in the bamboo's acclimatization period.[2]

A booming industry had developed through the 1980s that established global supply chains of plant material and sophisticated propagation and acclimatization procedures for indoor planting.[3] Maintaining the kind of extensive interior landscapes that were proliferating in atriums, especially in the northern hemisphere, required specialist knowledge beyond that of the architect or engineer. One commentator noted: "With indoor landscape being available for approximately the same capital cost as good quality hard landscape there is bound to be a growth in demand and a lack of people who know what they are doing."[4]

Technical advice for architects and facilities managers had begun circulating from the late 1970s. Richard Gaines's *Interior Plantscaping* (1977) and Stephen Scrivens's *Interior Planting in Large Buildings* (1980) were significant publications on either side of the Atlantic.[5] Scrivens wrote an extended series of articles for the *Architects' Journal*: a comprehensive overview of what it meant to plant a large-scale garden inside a building, followed by case studies of buildings in the United Kingdom, the United States, and Europe, several of which featured planted atriums.[6] Key to his approach was his conception of buildings as artificial environments. The science of plant physiology that had developed in the postwar period gave new emphasis to the environmental factors affecting plant growth,[7] from light levels, temperature, humidity, and air quality to structures and systems used to accommodate, support, and maintain plant life. What was adequate for humans might not be for plants, so much focus was given to plant acclimatization and the adaptation of different species to artificial environmental conditions. In his case studies Scrivens mostly saw failures of design, plant selection, lighting levels, drainage systems, and care and maintenance. Yet from this situation he managed to develop systematic, practical knowledge, not just of interior landscape design and maintenance, but more significantly of the environment buildings produced within their walls.

As the struggle of indoor plants attested, this environment revealed its artificiality every time a drainage duct failed, or an infestation of bugs took over.[8] "Nature" in the atrium was thus another form of what Francis Duffy called scenery, a construction within a building that served the accommodation requirements of tenants. The theatrical sense of this scenery is significant, because it acknowledges the representational effect of nature deployed as part of a narrative. It also has a domestic connotation, as representations of domestic interiors were historically part of the inventory of sets used in theater. Indeed, the term "interior" gained its modern, domestic meaning in this theatrical and representational sense.[9] Nature became a staged condition, and even clichéd impressions had an objective for organizations accommodating themselves in atrium buildings.

★★★

At Kevin Roche and John Dinkeloo's Ford Foundation headquarters in Manhattan (1968), landscape was invited within the architectural envelope in the most spectacular fashion. Far from maximizing the developable potential of the Midtown site—the building topped out at the point where New York City's early twentieth-century zoning law would have required a setback[10]—Roche and Dinkeloo provided an entirely different kind of value proposition for an organization ascendant in the cold war geopolitics of development and aid.

Square in plan, two slabs of twelve-story office accommodation defined the north and west boundaries of the site and framed a full-height atrium, with the south and east of the atrium enclosed by a glass curtain wall. The top two floors of the atrium were ringed by further office space just below a skylight. Immediately to the east was the garden of an adjacent apartment complex. This orientation provided the atrium an unencumbered vantage point and access to light, and the terraced landscape, with neat geometrical paths and stairs leading through, negotiated the change of level between 42nd and 43rd streets.

Figure 5.2 Ford Foundation, New York. Kevin Roche & John Dinkeloo, 1968 © Ezra Stoller / Esto.

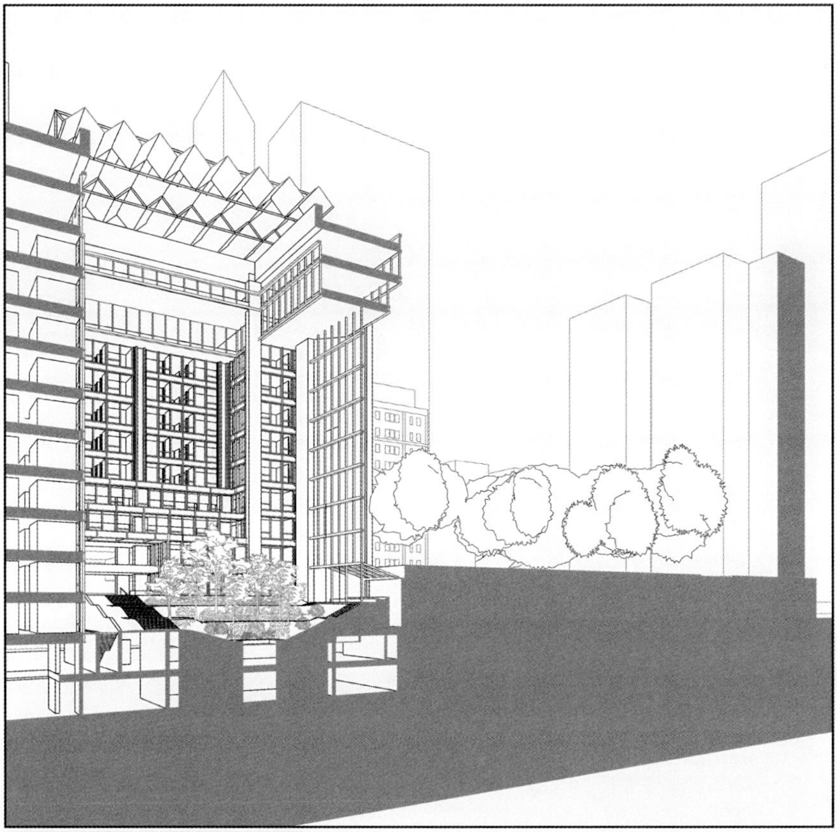

Figure 5.3 Ford Foundation, New York. Kevin Roche & John Dinkeloo, 1968. Drawing by Noah Gotlib, Oskar Johanson, and Sophie Lanigan.

The presence of the landscape in the building caused a disjunction of scale: the building itself seemed diminutive at only 12 stories, yet the atrium appeared massive at 156 feet in height, and a third of an acre in area.[11] These figures suggest that there was perhaps no appropriate measure for an architecturally enclosed landscape of this kind, except, perhaps, in its ability to incorporate an enormous amount of foliage: 20,000 plants were used to create it,[12] and the building's landscape architect, Dan Kiley, had hoped that the trees he specified, among them *Magnolia grandiflora*, might grow to the full height of the atrium.[13]

As David Gissen has argued, the atrium garden's influence on the rest of New York City was profound, being seen as a way to respond to concerns regarding the environmental quality of the city, which, deep in debt in the mid-1970s, was increasingly unable to develop or maintain its parks and gardens.[14] While Buckminster Fuller's 1960 proposal for a geodesic dome sealing Midtown Manhattan might have been the most audacious proposal to control the city's environment,[15] through the 1970s and '80s the Ford Foundation's interior landscape offered a spatial model for the Manhattan office tower, under pressure from the flight of corporations away from the city into suburban office parks, to be reimagined through a connection to "nature." The challenge posed by the office in the park would be met by the park in the office. As Gissen has noted, in the Ford Foundation's Midtown East neighborhood, around twenty enclosed gardens were proposed for new developments. About a dozen of these took advantage of a planning code that operated between 1970 and 1982, giving floor space bonuses to buildings incorporating covered and air-conditioned pedestrian spaces.[16] This represented an evolution of planning provisions, in operation since the early 1960s and revised in the mid-1970s, that had given floor space bonuses for the provision of outdoor plazas, a measure which took as its precedent the forecourt of Mies van der Rohe's Seagram Building (1958). Yet, within a decade, Roche and Dinkeloo's Ford Foundation effectively usurped it as the model for the production of privately owned public urban space in the city,[17] with the New York Botanical Garden, the stewarding institution of the city's outdoor parks and gardens, pivoting in its mission to support the corporate provision of interior landscapes.[18]

The Ford Foundation aspired to change the relationship between individual, organization, building, and city. Even before the building was complete, *Progressive Architecture* discussed the relationship between the kind of "man" who would be employed in the building—"people of unusually high academic caliber"—and the work they would do: "Since their work does not result in a 'visible' product as in a manufacturing company, it was necessary for the building to create the feeling of a community of common effort."[19] The feeling of "community" was brought about by a particular kind of visibility. Employees could look through into the atrium garden as well as across it to those working in other parts of the building. The *Progressive Architecture* review expanded this dynamic to include the building's connection to the city at large: "The relationship in scale is thus: man to the interior court, to the building as a whole, to the street outside, to the city itself. This is a relationship seldom experienced in other buildings, where man encounters an abrupt switch from the small scale of his office and elevator to the teeming street."[20] This account hinted at the "organization man" used to this kind of abrupt urban transition. Yet the Ford Foundation attempted to orient a new kind of subject in the city, the knowledge worker, and imagined that the building could enact and even symbolize what that kind of work meant within the organization, and in the city at large.

By the time the building was complete, *Progressive Architecture* was more confident in its pronouncements about the spatial positioning of this subject. Discussing the various ambiguous relationships between inside and outside in the building—the outside-inside of the atrium garden, the inside-outside of balcony spaces opening onto it, and the fact that office windows could be opened to the atrium but not to "outside"—the reviewer thought: "The building is an epitome of our age's awareness of and involvement in multiple levels of experience, and it suggests a comprehensive level of perception that measures architecture by a huge scale—one based on the city-scape rather than on images of single buildings."[21] Roche's own architect's statement put this in more prosaic terms, but nonetheless captured the sense in which the building was meant to operate as a kind of transformed panopticon, "a space that would allow [employees] to enjoy the view but at the same time allow them to be aware of the existence of other members of the Foundation, people who share their common aims and purposes—the family of effort to which they belong."[22]

Reviews since the building's completion have emphasized these visual qualities, as well as the building's supposed connection to nineteenth-century glasshouse structures. Michael Sorkin condemned the Ford Foundation as a "concatenation of Mies and the Crystal Palace, an eleemosynary hothouse, a frame for the cultivation of charity's bureaucracy."[23] Chiming in with Sorkin, Dan Graham and Robin Hurst also drew on a lineage of glass architecture and emphasized the private, surveilled nature of these new, proliferating "corporate arcadias," especially their attempt to "smooth over contradictions between environmental decay and technological progress."[24] Similarly, M. Christine Boyer, invoking John Ruskin's abhorrence of the Crystal Palace, argued that the Ford Foundation's image of benevolence and order ultimately abandoned the city outside its calm interior.[25] And in its geopolitical machinations, the Ford Foundation, in Felicity Scott's words, "stepped in to build new Crystal Palaces, those no longer displaying industrial goods, but revealing new operatives in an emergent neoimperial enterprise as it expanded under the opportunistic rubric of development aid, resource management, and security."[26]

In the invocation of the lineage of glasshouse architecture, the condition of the landscape within has been assumed to be one of flourishing, its "exotic" flora standing in for the archetypal, vaguely tropical "far off" that was nonetheless enfolded within the Ford Foundation and its mission. Expected to remain lush and replete, the landscape could be understood to signal a kind of false consciousness: a flourishing landscape signifying a flourishing organization, one that was deeply involved in developing new, engineered agricultural solutions in the so-called developing world. Any decay in the landscape itself could be seen to undo this signification and embarrass the organization.[27]

The garden did indeed suffer dramatically from plant loss and stunted growth within the first years of its establishment, and over time species originally planted were replaced by others more able to adapt to the rigors of the building's artificial environment.[28] Yet, as Danielle Choi has argued, Kiley had never intended that the landscape exist in a stable, flourishing condition, or that it represent the climate of particular regions, as some commentators assumed. Rather, plants' rates of survival, adaptation, and death all provided feedback on the nature of the environmental condition within the building, and thus on the ability of an organization of plants to coexist with a human organization.[29]

Kiley drew on the plant physiology of Frits Went, in particular his 1957 book *The Experimental Control of Plant Growth*. Went had developed the phytotron, a lab facility that maintained extremely precise environmental conditions whose individual parameters could be isolated and varied as part of the scientific experiments he conducted on plant growth.[30] Yet, having been built for human occupation, the Ford Foundation atrium was far from a phytotron. While the atrium itself was passively controlled, its environment ended up being too stable and unchanging, lacking the seasonal changes that are significant factors in plant growth.[31] To account for this, Kiley made use of horticultural knowledge developed by a contemporary of Went, the botanist Alfred Byrd Graf who worked for the commercial nursery Julius Roehrs and Company in New Jersey and who published *Exotica: Pictorial Cyclopedia of Indoor Plants* in the same year as Went's book. While Graf indulged in the kind of adventurism of his nineteenth-century forebears in seeking out plants that could do well indoors, he recognized that plant adaptation was the key.[32] It was not the exoticism of any species per se, nor even the supposed tropicality of an environment that could support them, but the fact that they could tolerate the rigors of the decidedly artificial, human-centered environment of the atrium. Everett Conklin, the horticulturalist who was contracted to install and maintain the landscape and whose firm, also based in New Jersey, was a competitor of Julius Roehrs and Company,[33] worked with Kiley on the selection of atrium plants,[34] moving between the frames of the scientific, the aesthetic, and the economic. Choi has written of this intersection: "Like weeds, so-called ornamental plants are neither a taxonomic nor biological category—human desire, markets and cultivation define their dispersal, reproduction, and range."[35]

In this way the garden in the atrium of the Ford Foundation did not remain an absolutely stable signifier of the Foundation's role, nor did it totally break down to reveal this as false consciousness. Rather, the garden existed as a living organization, one developed and maintained over time via processes of trial and error in much the same way the Foundation approached the financial management of its philanthropic task.[36] "Human desire, markets and cultivation" seem like apt descriptors for the factors governing the Foundation's work, mapping onto "the opportunistic rubric of development aid, resource management, and security."[37] They are also apt descriptors of the domestic context of the horticultural industry Graf and Conklin were part of.

This was a point seized on by Kenneth Frampton in his review of the building published at the time of its completion. For Frampton, the Ford Foundation was "the patio house solution on a colossal scale, eccentrically extended in height."[38] As one entered into what he called the "patio-conservatory," "one may take a very constricted turn around the 'garden,' gape briefly at the greenery, at the vast space above, watch the diligent 'family workers' behind their hermetic glass, and then leave—for other than going up for a 'grant' or a 'guided tour,' there is nothing else to do and no point of arrival or rest."[39] While the garden might have been publicly accessible, there was no reason for an outsider to be there. Frampton thought that the excessive domestic garden was an "anti-agora,"[40] and that there was more public, urban amenity to be found in the average bank lobby. He asked: "Are we to conclude from this that in our Western society, the house of private profit is more naturally rendered 'public' than the house of private, non-profit, public benevolence?"[41] The building remained a profoundly introverted one, signaling, for Frampton, insecurity rather than confidence. "The public, like the more ordinary objects of our industrial civilization, must be ministered to, but kept constantly at a distance. It is a wholly regrettable but highly dangerous symbolic stance for a great benevolent institution to adopt."[42]

★★★

When Herman Hertzberger (with Lucas & Niemeijer) completed the offices for the cooperative insurance company Centraal Beheer in 1972, the company moved from Amsterdam to the provincial town of Apeldoorn, about 100 kilometers to the east. It was not quite the shift of a skyscraper-bound US corporation to the verdant, horizontal suburbs, yet it created an opportunity for the company to change the way employees related to their work environment.[43] Again crucial in this was the role of plants in an atrium, this time actual pot plants that required employees' personal care and attention.

Designed to accommodate around 1,000 employees, the Centraal Beheer Office Building was structured, quite literally, as a three-dimensional, concrete grid. From the exterior, the building appeared as a series of stacked boxes rising from two levels at its edges to four levels at its center. In the interior this grid arranged a repeating element: a nine-by-nine-meter unit that could be configured in various ways to function as office space with gradations of openness and privacy, or to contain ancillary functions. The units were grouped into four quadrants arranged in a pinwheel formation and separated by top-lit voids. Each quadrant was designed to contain a range of public functions, including eating, meeting, and shopping places. These were linked together by entry-level "streets" that were open to the public. The building's atrium condition was created through the distribution of voids between the office quadrants, and in a larger, full-height void at their meeting point. This was certainly not the monumental, singular atrium of the Ford Foundation, or any number of similar examples, but

Figure 5.4 Centraal Beheer Office Building, Apeldoorn, The Netherlands. Herman Hertzberger, 1972. Photograph by Herman Hertzberger. Courtesy Herman Hertzberger.

rather a distributed, imbricated one. It did, however, exhibit similarly complex spatial and visual effects.

The voids set up a dynamic of privacy and semi-enclosure, as well as one of cohesion and connection between the different parts of the building, both across levels and between them. This has been described in terms of the building's "city" ambitions, with the folding-in of public and social functions along its streets, and its multiple entrance points. Francis Duffy commented on the way in which "the full height central space is not only the place for most vertical circulation but also the social centre of the entire building where there are several coffee bars and a great many places to sit. On a bright day with shafts of sunlight from the rooflight contrasting with shadowed alcoves, the scale is perfect, with all the most attractive connotations of the Mediterranean village street."[44]

Because the building enabled separation as well as connection, Alan Colquhoun saw that its overall arrangement tackled problems with both cellularized office layouts and the legacy of Bürolandschaft.[45] He situated it within an emerging interest in buildings as self-regulating systems, whereby "it is the user who plays the active role in the building, while the architect's role is rather to provide the framework that allows the user to choose his own behavior. The well-being of the user is the result of his own spontaneous activity and not of any forms imposed on his environment by the architect."[46] Architectural imposition, or its lack, however, remained a contested issue. The building's materiality was a point of focus for several critics, with the interior of exposed concrete structure and gray-block infill perhaps demanding embellishment, and Hertzberger would have agreed that the literal structure of the building and the use of repetitive though flexible units offered an incitement to such user engagement.[47]

As several contemporary critics noted, this engagement was most visible through the houseplants that employees were encouraged to bring in to work. While Hertzberger himself would promote the user as co-designer, Graham Moss described what he saw as the crucial role of an organizational intermediary, Centraal Beheer's office manager W. M. Jansen: "His ability to instill confidence into the executives, while giving Hertzberger his inventive freedom, played a more vital role in the design process than most architectural critics are keen to admit." Client and architect were able "to define the future direction of an organization and to develop an appropriate building solution and image, around which organization and work patterns have been able to rearrange themselves."[48] This rearrangement, together with users' own "spontaneous activity," took more extreme forms than expected, with aviaries and fish tanks added by staff.[49] Coupled with this exuberant expression, though, was a higher-than-expected staff turnover of those used to a more traditionally regulated work environment. With what was described as a "carefully monitored recruitment system," however, staff attrition was apparently reduced over time.[50]

The supposed free play of individual expression and employee engagement begins to look somewhat constrained, if not suspect. For his part, Colquhoun was unsure whether plants were brought in by employees or provided by the building management.[51] In his detailed examination of the interior planting, Stephen Scrivens confirmed that it was a combination of both. He described how a maintenance officer was employed to take care of the supplied plants—mostly houseplant varieties—that were grown in specially installed planters, and individual workers were given responsibility for the plants that they brought into their work areas. He observed a deal of variation in standards of plant care, but those that were well tended were destined for greater things. Scrivens wrote:

> One complaint about the building is that the architect failed to allow enough space for planting to grow. The problem is made more serious because the plant maintenance officer has a policy of not cutting back plants and prefers to move large plants into area where they can grow still further. . . . If a "personalized" plant becomes too successful, the plant maintenance officer moves it to a more suitable location and a replacement is purchased to make good the loss.[52]

There was a tacit collective effort, albeit managed by a "maintenance officer," to try to organize the relationship between plants and building as a proxy for the employees' own "autonomous" relation to the building and the company they worked for. In this instance plants were signifiers of occupation, of participation in the ideology of individual appropriation of space. Those plants that stood out—those that flourished as a result of more participatory engagement—were allowed more space or more conducive environmental conditions in a regime that appropriated that very care and autonomy. Scrivens noted a further, unseen infrastructure of collective control, one that had to do with pests: "Even privately supplied plants are removed from desks and collected in the nearest public area for treatment to eliminate as far as possible all sources of reinfestation."[53]

While he was initially charmed by the building's village-like impression, the issue, for Duffy, was what the signs of all this user engagement ultimately meant: "Could it be that the whole building is an enormous red herring, cynically erected by management to divert worker attention from real issues? By permitting at very small expense a certain amount of autonomous interior decoration, has management bought peace and the reputation for being progressive?" And he went further: "If there had been really serious labour problems, real grievances, real exploitation . . . would Hertzberger's intervention have been the cure or an aggravation?"[54] The answer was moot, but by asking such a pointed series of questions Duffy indicated that he was struggling to assign a value to the building's system of user engagement.

Similarly, Colquhoun was troubled by what the building's overt systematization actually meant for architecture:

> [Hertzberger] seems here to align himself with the *grands simplificateurs* of the modern movement for whom architecture is simply the demonstration of some internal principle, of a "system" that automatically ensures virtue in the same way photosynthesis in a plant creates beauty. But there is no

> guarantee, in man-made objects, that a unitary principle, similar to what can be deduced from the biochemistry of plant life will result in the wonderful variety found in nature. The puritanical fear of "making an impression" may blind one to the fact that all buildings make an impression—Hertzberger's not least—and the problem is to decide *what* impression needs to be made.[55]

Colquhoun was clearly worried about the supposed self-evidence—the virtue—of the building's systems logic in much the same way Duffy was worried about it from an organizational perspective. The two modes of organization, the literally organic mode of the system of plants and the metaphorically organic one of the building's spatial and structural system, were coincident. Whatever impression the building was making was being made by the occupants and their "occupation."

That impression occasioned debate when the building was put before a panel of architects and critics, including Stanford Anderson, Peter Eisenman, John Hejduk, Leon Krier, and Robert Stern, at a conference titled "Beyond the Modern Movement" held at Harvard University in 1977. Centraal Beheer was one of six architectural projects discussed, amongst others by Michael Graves, Arata Isozaki, Charles Moore, Aldo Rossi, and Venturi and Rauch.[56]

Centraal Beheer was presented with a brief description and a short text from Hertzberger's "The Building as Instrument for Its Occupants" of 1973, and then discussed in relation to two other projects: Charles Moore's postmodern Whitman Village Housing in Long Island, New York (1974), and Aldo Rossi's rationalist Residential Unit in the Gallaratese Quarter in Milan (1974). The cluster of buildings immediately threw into relief issues of signification and meaning, and these were given a straightforward definition by Stern: "the idea that buildings can have semantic importance, that they can address things other than simply how they are put together or what literally happens inside them."[57]

Eisenman launched the discussion with the following observation: "One of the problems in evaluating these projects is the rhetoric in relationship to the reality. The thing that disturbs me most about Hertzberger's building is its extreme geometric determinism. The building consists of little boxes piled on boxes. If that's antimonumental then the work has no meaning."[58] For Eisenman, this was part of the larger issue of the way in which signification worked. Any system of signification in architecture was, at best, arbitrary: "There is no way of making a correlation between a building and 'humanity' or 'inhumanity.'"[59] What was troubling was that Hertzberger, in Eisenman's eyes, was attempting to make just this correlation.

Stern chimed in with a blunter version of that critique: "Hertzberger's building is not merely a piece of geometry . . . he also says that because it is a rather bleak piece of geometry, you have to bring in your plants from home. The architect has given up on doing anything to the environment beyond providing a place which the user has to brighten up. You'd have to spend all day just watering the plants within that building."[60] Anderson, though, countered Eisenman's critique that the building was just a series of "repetitive units," asking what such a repetition might produce in the context of the building being an office. He noted its fundamental difference from the usual flat floorplates regularly encountered in this type and wondered what the effect of that might be for the way the building functioned. But Stern doubled down on his critique, arguing along with Eisenman that the very fact that user intervention was demanded meant that the building itself lacked an answer to Anderson's question: "Hertzberger says that you must bring in your entire world of signification, of decoration, of inhabitation, into your office. The architecture gives you nothing, *just* a place, in that sense."[61] Whitman Village and the Gallaratese housing were at least residential structures, the question of architectural versus personal signification being an inherent tension in that type.

What emerged through the Harvard discussion was a conundrum: the modernist rhetoric of function had been displaced by questions of user engagement. And that displacement was itself rhetorical. As Eisenman argued, it was an issue of the architect's words as against the building's formal presence. A gap existed between the two, and it seemed disingenuous to Eisenman and Stern that it be filled by the building user expressing their mode of inhabitation. Any signification that architecture should be able to project, whether unconsciously or self-consciously, had been ceded to the inhabitants and their potted plants. In this respect even the architectural ambition of the Ford Foundation was lost. Both buildings were, in effect, domestic structures.

★★★

By the time the Harvard conference took place, Stern's sense of "semantic importance" was best understood in relation to stylistic postmodernism, the idea, not exactly new, that buildings could speak directly to culture via signs and symbols. Terry Farrell's TV-am Headquarters in London (1982) was, in stylistic terms, the highest of high postmodernism, and Farrell had no qualms about what impression his building needed to make. The design converted and augmented an existing 1930s industrial building backing onto Regent's Canal in Camden to provide production studios and offices for a television station that had been granted a new license to broadcast morning news and current affairs programming across the United Kingdom. Extending to the edges of the two-acre site, the structure contained parking and studios on the ground level, and editorial offices in a mix of cellular and open-plan arrangements on a level above. An existing sawtooth roof carried over the entire structure, and running through the middle was a wedge-shaped void that was turned into an atrium, providing entry, reception, and circulation space. A monumental stair linked both levels, and a bridge carried across the upper level, joining the two sides of offices. Because of the depth of the building's plan, the atrium was crucial in providing a sense of focus and openness of view in a building with few external windows.

The atrium contained what Farrell described as a "world village." Arranged through furniture, freestanding structures, and planting was "a

Figure 5.5 TV-am Headquarters, London. Terry Farrell, 1982 Richard Bryant / ARCAID.

Mediterranean area with fig trees," a canal "decorated in Venetian style," a "Middle East/Babylonian ziggurat," and "at the very Far East we have a little Temple of Chinese and Japanese abstraction."[62] One critic noted the way in which the atrium created "an infinitely extensible fantasy world at the centre of the building."[63] The atrium ran east-west across the site, and the sawtooth roof provided morning sun from the east. Farrell recounts: "We fixed on this east west symbolism, and also the idea that all the world's news is being gathered here, and decided to do a round the world garden."[64] Signification, here, was literal, if somewhat kitsch and culturally reductive. Where, in a high modern sense, the Ford Foundation's signification of an elsewhere could be read as false consciousness, TV-am Headquarters pointed to the very gestures it was making. Everything was literally scenery: "world garden" as televisual backdrop.

TV-am had been set up when the UK's Independent Broadcasting Authority offered a new franchise for nationwide morning news and current affairs programming. A group of high-profile television journalists, including David Frost and Michael Parkinson, were awarded the franchise and established the company in 1980, broadcasting beginning on 1 February 1983. Farrell had to conjure the organization out of nothing.[65] The very nature of his approach to the project, a speedy renovation of an existing building, had to do with the deadline for being on air.[66] The building was constructed via a new instrument that had gained traction with the deregulation of the architectural profession: the design-build contract. The building's eclecticism was as much to do with how the contracting was structured as it was a conscious design decision. Farrell as architect negotiated separate budgets for the facades and interior and had different teams working on each.[67]

Notwithstanding this business-minded approach, Farrell had been shortlisted to design the headquarters because, in the words of one of TV-am's founders, Michael Deakin, "his buildings make me laugh. . . . TV-am is in show business. We are not civil servants. We are actors and clowns, and clowns need circus tents; in a sense this building is our circus tent. It has a very important message. Most people don't get buildings that reflect the character of their organizations, and this one does just that, and it makes it a better place to work."[68] If the aesthetics were entirely alien, and the relationship between client and architect were expressed in a less than serious way, there were still strong echoes from the ethos of Centraal Beheer. Farrell argued that his design "wasn't a glass block corporate building, . . . but something that contained all the elements of a village or a mini city. The looseness, the relaxedness, the accidental happenings were given a role and were not over-controlled."[69]

Despite claims to this kind of looseness, Centraal Beheer operated through an apparatus of engagement. Plants and their care and maintenance were a proxy for the relationship between employee and company and provided a way to structure it. The atrium voids made that relationship visible to all. Similarly, at TV-am Headquarters, while the world garden provided a "fun" backdrop, the central stair and bridge that punctuated the atrium space took on an important organizational role. Critics and Farrell himself recognized that the stair in particular functioned as the main element of circulation between the different parts of the building and was a "control point" between executive offices above and the television studios below. It also acted as a position from which all staff could be addressed over the building's two levels.[70] There was an echo of the panoptic qualities noticed in the Ford Foundation, and this is the other aspect of the building as stage set: not only its facilitation of broadcast television across the United Kingdom, but the production—and control—of a particular kind of organizational dynamic within. These were two sides of the same coin.

From its first broadcast the company was beset by organizational and financial woes as well as fluctuating ratings. By 1984 Australian media tycoon Kerry Packer had bought a stake in the company and one of his executives, Bruce Gyngell, became managing director.[71] Gyngell, the first man to appear on television in Australia, purported to run "a family and familiar organisation" projecting a "cosy relaxed atmosphere."[72] The problems continued, however, with regulators reprimanding the station for poor investment in their news coverage, which risked their retention of the license. By 1987 a strike by technical staff led to an extended lockout by Gyngell, who sacked them the following year.[73] The station would lose its license and close in 1992, the result of new legislation brought in by Thatcher's government. TV licenses were to be auctioned to the highest bidder, with TV-am losing out to Sunrise Television.

Duffy had wondered whether Centraal Beheer's user engagement should be understood as a cynical gesture, and at TV-am Headquarters his fears were realized. The atrium's bridge and stair controlled these chaotic labor relations while its clichéd scenery attempted to distract from them. These were the brutal machinations at the core of an industry deregulated in order to promote innovations such as "morning television." The sun would rise across homes in the United Kingdom as it did over a building that was organized around an ersatz scene of this very occurrence. Viewers who tuned in on the morning of 9 June 1985 would have seen David Frost interview Margaret Thatcher on his program *Frost on Sunday* and hear him ask the Prime Minister: "Is what we see on the television the real you?" Thatcher replied that she struggled somewhat with the disjunction she experienced between her sense of self and her media presentation, replying: "I am very nervous and it is not until I lose myself in an argument that I really am quite natural."[74] By argument, she meant the debate of policies. Almost exactly thirty years later, on the other side of the Atlantic, in a marble and mirror atrium, a former reality TV star would understand political argument to mean "fight," the clash of persona it involved by then fully domesticated by the media of news as entertainment.

★★★

The insertion of various forms of "nature" in these atriums relied on domestic tropes, from patio house to potted plants to interior set. Each was the backdrop, the scenery for narratives framing the relationship between employee and organization, narratives that could be positioned along a spectrum from the idealistic to the cynical. The atrium allowed these insertions because it was an insertion itself, a material condition in excess of, or indifferent to, the functional or symbolic conditions of the type of building that enclosed it. Aside from technical and aesthetic commentary on the highly constructed "nature" of these insertions, their critical interpretation belied a disciplinary anxiety.

At the Ford Foundation, architecture's urban presence was seen to be diminished by the building managing inadequately the relationship between public and private. There were concerns about how Centraal Beheer was meant to signify as architecture if it was simply a geometric structure awaiting finishing touches provided by employees. And at TV-am Headquarters a stage-set approach playfully represented the context of media production.

The source of this anxiety and confusion was the idea that what had been brought inside was a different—and probably misplaced—version of architecture: the domestic in the place of work, the private in place of the public. In each case, however, this domesticity materialized as a version of nature adopted for organizationally strategic purposes: the experimental garden naturalizing the geopolitics of risk and resource, the individually tended garden personalizing transactional relationships, and the clichéd garden distracting from deregulation itself.

This takes us back to the way in which the origin of the atrium building was located amidst the tension between what has been considered to be internal and what external to architecture as a discipline. The computational basis of the court form enabled architecture to formalize the externally imposed parameters of regulation, codification, and technical performance that would increasingly govern how buildings came into being. At the same time modes of calculating and assessing performance were also being internalized within the organizations that called upon atrium buildings to accommodate their needs. Equally important was the relationship between building user and building use, or to put this in more specific terms, between employee and the material conditions of their employment. As employees became increasingly responsible for their own performance, atrium buildings offered the means of more sophisticated forms of "personal" engagement, versions of domesticated nature being called upon to materialize this engagement. Employees related primarily to the nature these atriums contained, rather than to the buildings as architecture, and this short-circuited architecture's disciplinary modes of technique and signification.

While the maintenance of an atrium garden might be considered to be the apogee of the technical efforts to provide a "livable" indoor environment at scale, efforts that drew upon architecture's embrace of calculation and performance, this was shown to be the triumph of the interior as a staged condition. The fear was that behind the scenery that now did the job of mediating the social and political relationships of work, architecture was, at best, a scaffold, a flexible structure that could be relied on to make the "best use of land"[75] but that, in the end, could only point to this achievement as, quite literally, a form of hollowness.

Epilogue: The Atrium Persists

At the time of writing this epilogue, Helmut Jahn's State of Illinois Center, also known as the James R. Thompson Center (1985), had just been purchased by Google with a view to renovating it as their second building in Chicago. The building's squat, chamfered form encloses a 17-story, top-lit, cylindrical atrium, and its color palette of coral red and pastel blue seems ready-made for Google as it attempts to accommodate the needs of what it calls its "flexible hybrid workforce."[1] The history of this building acts as something of an encapsulation of the themes of this book, and the building's potential future offers a way of reflecting on the atrium's role in framing architecture's ongoing transformations since the late twentieth century.

The Thompson Center initially arrived as something of an oddity in Chicago's Loop, looking askance at its governmental counterparts across the street, Holabird & Root's neoclassical Chicago City Hall (1911) and C. F. Murphy Associates' Cor-Ten-clad Richard J. Daley Center (1965). The Thompson Center and its two neighbors convey the history of approaches to the relationship between building form and city grid, and between government and citizen, across the twentieth century.[2] Punctuated by two interior courts, City Hall meets each edge of its block with gigantic colonnaded facades, the Daley Center steps back from a vast open plaza after the example of Mies, while the Thompson Center carves an entirely different space out of the city, a great, angled curve slicing the corner off its form and opening the atrium, via a full-height glazed facade, to a wedge of exterior plaza. This urban gesture is a lesson in inside/outside ambiguity, the building's reflective facade rebuffing the presentational clarity of its neighbors, while inviting the public into an urban-scaled space at once grander and more bewildering than anything outside. A metro station below opens onto a sunken food court and shops at the piazza-like base of the atrium, with the exposed elevator shafts that service the open office floorplates above offering a dramatic, kinetic spectacle.

As Joanna Merwood-Salisbury has shown, reviewers of the building lined up on either side of a debate over the qualities of dazzle versus those of decorum. While some found in the atrium a refreshing model for civic monumentality, others saw only vulgarity in what was considered to be an unholy mix of government building and shopping mall, ersatz and kitsch taking the place of genuine public engagement.[3] One critic characterized it as a "fractured space," likening its effects to the "temporal and spatial disjunctions" of the "Sony Walkman" and "popular electronic media."[4] Jahn was seen either as a consummate producer of images, or as someone who mocked the very idea of architectural representation.[5] Michael Sorkin also weighed in with a short review that suggested Jahn had redeemed the atrium form by imbuing it with a public function. The atrium was still inherently evil—Sorkin took the opportunity in his review to decry Portman's hotels and suggested that atriums "poach on the life of urban streets, our most cherished public space, and thus sap their cities"[6]—but he did acknowledge that the form was "where the action is."[7]

Heralded at its inception in 1980 as a "building for the year 2000," the Thompson Center projected no small sense of its own historical importance,[8] yet the real "action" of the building was situated within the practical, professional domain of architectural services, the embedding of which has been the focus of this book. Rather than immediately emphasizing

Figure 6.1 James R. Thompson Center, Chicago. Helmut Jahn, 1985. Photograph by the author.

its aesthetic and experiential qualities, Jahn announced, soberly, that the building would be constructed with "a balanced approach to first cost and life cycle costs, a concern for the conservation of energy, and a flexibility for future change."[9] A significant aspect of the project was the structure of its procurement, which reflected the realities of specialized, corporatized practice. While Jahn was the publicized author, the State of Illinois's Capital Development Board contracted a series of consultants to deliver the project. The building was designed and documented through a joint venture between C. F. Murphy Associates—the firm becoming Murphy/Jahn during its construction—and Lester B. Knight Associates. The interior design and space planning were handled under a separate contract by Vickery/Ovresat/Awsumb Associates who undertook an extensive client liaison process that was aided by a bespoke computer planning program. The construction management firm of Morse/Diesel oversaw the integration of inputs across the project.[10]

The Thompson Center also responded to regulatory and technological issues that had become familiar by the 1980s. One commentator noted that there would be "cries of envy at the latitude of the fire regulations in force."[11] Energy and environmental performance was particularly prominent in the building's design, and it was the subject of an analysis by the College of Environmental Design at the University of California, Berkeley, through a program funded by the US Department of Energy.[12] The analysis concluded that the building's mechanical systems would be crucial to its energy performance. During the first years of the building's operation, however, the innovative HVAC design, which featured ice tanks in place of the usual chiller technology, proved to be seriously flawed, with temperatures reaching scorching highs in summer.[13] Its sophisticated control mechanism was difficult to manage, and energy-saving glazing had been cut from the specification due to cost issues.[14] The risks associated with these innovations lay with the architects and, inevitably, ended up in multiple lawsuits. The HVAC system was upgraded in 1987, and the state sued Murphy/Jahn and Lester B. Knight Associates, claiming that they had been negligent in the design and installation of the system. Murphy/Jahn launched a countersuit against Knight, claiming the joint venture agreement meant that Knight was the firm responsible for the design of the HVAC system. Knight, in turn, sued several contractors over the system's installation.[15] Organizationally, noise and privacy were also significant problems, as the office floors were open to the atrium, which often featured lunchtime events. And, in an extreme heightening of the visual qualities of the open floorplates, binoculars were said to have been used to survey employees.[16]

Over time, the state became increasingly concerned about poor building performance, rising operating costs, and mounting bills for deferred maintenance, and decided to sell the building in 2015.[17] Legislative approval for the sale was only granted in 2019, and in the intervening period a preservation campaign was launched and garnered support from Docomomo US, the Society of Architectural Historians, the American Institute of Architects, the National Trust for Historic Preservation, and ICOMOS's International Scientific Committee on Historic Preservation, all of which urged landmark designation based on the building being an "icon" of postmodern architecture and significant in the public monumentality provided by its atrium.[18] That bid ultimately proved unsuccessful, but the efforts point to the fact that "one of the generic building forms of the late twentieth century"[19] had become historical.

Preservation and reuse have become the dominant modes by which this becoming-historical of the atrium building has been recognized and acted upon. The Ford Foundation headquarters was given Interior Landmark status by the City of New York in 1997.[20] The whole building was refurbished by Gensler, and the atrium garden redesigned by Raymond Jungles in 2018.[21] 1 Finsbury Avenue was given a Grade II heritage listing by Historic England in 2015 primarily for its facade,[22] with the building's interior being fully refurbished by AHMM in 2019. The Centraal Beheer Office Building fell into disuse and disrepair in the 2010s, and in mid-2022 became the subject of a plan to convert it into a residential development,

Herman Hertzberger collaborating with MVRDV on the design.[23] Jahn weighed in on the fate of the Thompson Center, proposing in 2015 to add a tower containing hotel and apartments to the site to make its redevelopment financially viable, and in 2020 he proposed turning the atrium into an open public space surrounded by "flexible tech offices . . . a hotel and co-living apartments."[24]

For its part, Google's statements about its intentions for the Thompson Center are the same as those that Jahn made at the inception of the project in 1980. Where he framed its significance in terms of "the conservation of energy, and a flexibility for future change," Google has promised to achieve "Class A" environmental performance and to "meet the future needs of [its] flexible, hybrid workforce."[25] In other words, Google has pledged to engage with the broader lessons the atrium has bequeathed to architecture: not the guarantee of superior energy performance or organizational effectiveness, but an ability to project these as architectural and organizational innovations couched in a framework of professional expertise.[26] Where the state failed, Google may show the way.

These statements might be dismissed as peripheral to what will no doubt be a continuing debate regarding the building's significance, and about its impact on the economy and the experience of Chicago's Loop, as the disjunctions of the Sony Walkman are superseded by the ubiquity of data and a public building becomes a private one. Yet these statements, Jahn's in 1980 and Google's in 2022, come to the heart of the atrium's historical significance. They show that the atrium has changed the terms by which such a judgment of significance might be made. Instead of being framed by the conventional categories of stylistic, aesthetic, functional, social, typological, or urban achievement, these statements relate to a different set of concerns that marked the emergence and proliferation of the atrium, those of technical expertise in place of disciplinary erudition, building performance in place of architectural importance, spatial indeterminacy in place of programmatic intention, and organizational strategy in place of user accommodation. Jahn's own professional persona notwithstanding, ultimately these concerns deny a valorization of the intentions of architects above those of other professionals who contribute to the making and maintenance of buildings. Or rather, as Jahn well knew, they position the architect as a professional in pursuit of business opportunity, "authorial" presence becoming a key strategy.[27]

The atrium's significance can be understood in the way it has enabled the emergence and persistence of these more intangible concerns in architecture. Indeed, it is a form of significance that is evidenced by the Thompson Center's failure in conventional terms, a failure framed by a business-minded desire for technical innovation that went hand in hand with its counterpart, the structure of risk management that was dealt with in this instance via litigation. Google's purchase of the Thompson Center doesn't simply represent the possibility of fixing the building's problems, but of understanding it as replete with the same kinds of professional and organizational possibilities that can be projected into a future marked by indeterminacy. In this way the atrium persists as "one of the generic building forms of the late twentieth century," framing a range of techniques for processing the distinction between inside and outside. Whether Google preserves the Thompson Center's atrium in its current form, changes it dramatically, or even fills it in, makes no difference in terms of the possibilities the atrium offers. Each would be a legitimate strategic approach to the material conditions of the existing atrium, and the organizational needs projected for the building. Preservation of the kind desired by the groups supporting the Thompson Center's listing would, in the event, acknowledge a particular set of professional and organizational interests, as well as social and political ones, over others.

Seen in this wider context, perhaps preservation is, as Rem Koolhaas has suggested, a form of strategic retreat for architecture in the face of transformations, beginning in the late twentieth century, that are still finding a conceptual framework appropriate to them.[28] In its own way, this book has been an attempt to contribute to this framework for architecture, with the atrium as its symbolic and material figure.

Acknowledgments

Research for this book was made possible by a Discovery Project grant from the Australian Research Council ("Urban Interiors: Architectural Change and the City since the 1960s," DP190101114). I am immensely grateful to Helen Gyger for her research assistance as part of that project. She showed considerable skill and tenacity in tracking down disparate material and carefully assembling it. Sophie Lanigan produced drawings and other visual material for the project with great perseverance. Oskar Johanson and Yvette Salmon provided valuable assistance.

Dean Hawkes and Richard Saxon generously gave their time to talk to me about their pioneering work on atrium buildings. I am grateful to Daniel Barber, Elizabeth Mossop, Barbara Penner, and Amy Thomas who read and commented on chapters in draft form. Sam Jacoby, Stephen Cairns, Isabelle Doucet, Daniel Koch, Liz Wayktus, Anthony Paletta, Tijana Stevanović, Barnabas Calder, Alex Bremner, Neal Shasore, Savia Palate, James Curry, David Kroll, and Liam Ross provided important and stimulating occasions for the discussion of work in progress. Mark Morris and Silvana Taher gave me the opportunity to teach this material as a seminar at the Architectural Association School of Architecture, and I am grateful to the students for their commitment and insights. The Faculty of Design,

Architecture and Building at the University of Technology Sydney supported the project through a subvention to defray the cost of images, and I am grateful to dean Elizabeth Mossop who provided a period of research leave at a crucial stage in the project. The book was completed as part of a Fulbright Scholarship at Taubman College of Architecture and Urban Planning at the University of Michigan, and I am indebted to dean Jonathan Massey for his hospitality and support.

At the MIT Press, Thomas Weaver saw potential in the project from an early stage and was a wise and encouraging guide. Matthew Abbate and Zhengyang Hua were meticulous editors. Mikhaela Rodwell has been my most incisive reader and the most wonderful, generous, and supportive partner throughout the project. This is *1983*, and it's for you, my love.

Notes

Prologue

1. Michael Sorkin, "Introduction: Variations on a Theme Park," in *Variations on a Theme Park: The New American City and the End of Public Space*, ed. Michael Sorkin (New York: Hill and Wang, 1992), xiii.

2. Sorkin, "Introduction: Variations on a Theme Park," xiii.

3. See the critiques of *Variations on a Theme Park* in Rosalyn Deutsche, *Evictions: Art and Spatial Politics* (Cambridge, MA: MIT Press, 1996), 283–284, including her description of the book's cover in terms of Renaissance figurative depictions; Paul Hirst, review of *Variations on a Theme Park: The New American City and the End of Public Space*, *AA Files* 25 (1993): 97–98; and my account in Charles Rice, *Interior Urbanism: Architecture, John Portman and Downtown America* (London: Bloomsbury, 2016), 99–100.

4. Fredric Jameson, *Postmodernism, or, the Cultural Logic of Late Capitalism* (Durham: Duke University Press, 1991), 40.

5. Jameson, *Postmodernism*, 39–40.

6. Jameson, *Postmodernism*, 43.

7. Jameson, *Postmodernism*, 42.

8. Jameson, *Postmodernism*, 44.

9. Jameson, *Postmodernism*, 38.

10. This summarizes my account of Jameson and the Bonaventure Hotel in Rice, *Interior Urbanism*, 20–26.

11. Jerold Kayden, *Privately Owned Public Space: The New York City Experience* (New York: John Wiley & Sons, 2000), 176.

12. Mary McLeod, "Architecture and Politics in the Reagan Era: From Postmodernism to Deconstructivism," *Assemblage* 8 (1989): 55.

13. Mike Davis, "Urban Renaissance and the Spirit of Postmodernism," *New Left Review* 151 (1985): 109–110. See also Mike Davis, "Fortress Los Angeles: The Militarization of Urban Space," in Sorkin, *Variations on a Theme Park*, 154–180.

14. Rice, *Interior Urbanism*, 20–26.

15. Kenny Cupers, Catharina Gabrielsson, and Helena Mattsson, "Introduction: Undead Neoliberalisms," in *Neoliberalism on the Ground: Architecture and Transformation from the 1960s to the Present*, ed. Cupers, Gabrielsson, and Mattsson (Pittsburgh: University of Pittsburgh Press, 2020), 5.

16. Sylvia Lavin, *Architecture Itself and Other Postmodernization Effects* (Montreal: Canadian Centre for Architecture, 2020).

17. Reinhold Martin, *Utopia's Ghost: Architecture and Postmodernism, Again* (Minneapolis: University of Minnesota Press, 2010), xi–xii.

18. Portman remains inextricable from the discussion of Jameson in Martin, *Utopia's Ghost*, 21, 36, 38, 74–76, 91, 106–108, 113, 169. The limitations of Jameson's critique of Portman are discussed by Lavin, *Architecture Itself*, 136–141; and Phillip R. Denny, "Pro-forma for a 1,500-Room Convention Hotel," in Lavin, *Architecture Itself*, 60–62. In his account of a contemporary, neoliberal architecture of affect, Douglas Spencer has reanimated Jameson's account of architecture's mediating function, especially as it relates to what he calls "atrial spaces." Douglas Spencer, *The Architecture of Neoliberalism: How Contemporary Architecture Became an Instrument of Control and Compliance* (London: Bloomsbury, 2016), 158. Of course, my own work has had a significant focus on Portman. See Rice, *Interior Urbanism*, which provided the impetus for the present study.

19. Bernhard Siegert, *Cultural Techniques: Grids, Filters, Doors, and Other Articulations of the Real*, trans. Geoffrey Winthrop-Young (New York: Fordham University Press, 2015), 9. Daniel Barber has used Siegert's formulation to describe how the architectural facade worked historically within modernism as a mediating device between the exterior environment and the thermal conditions within a building. Daniel Barber, *Modern Architecture and Climate: Design before Air Conditioning* (Princeton: Princeton University Press, 2020), 19. See also the use of the concept in terms of material devices of urban ordering in Reinhold Martin, *The Urban Apparatus: Mediapolitics and the City* (Minneapolis: University of Minnesota Press, 2016), 26–27.

20. Richard Saxon, *Atrium Buildings: Development and Design* (London: Architectural Press, 1983), 1.

21. See the website https://www.atriumbuildings.com/ for a geolocated list of around 200 atrium buildings constructed between 1960 and 1990. The website was put together as part of the research project from which this present study derives.

22. It is worth noting that significant atrium buildings were developed for a range of different types. Examples of housing include Eero Saarinen's Hill College House at the University of Pennsylvania (1960), John Portman's Antoine Graves Houses, Atlanta (1965), Louis Kahn's Erdman Hall at Bryn Mawr College, Pennsylvania (1965), Diamond & Myers's Housing Union Building (HUB), University of Alberta, Canada (1971), and Bertrand Goldberg's River City II, Chicago (1986). Examples of educational, institutional, and cultural buildings include Frank Lloyd Wright's Solomon R. Guggenheim Museum, New York (1959), John Andrews's Scarborough College, Canada (1964), João Vilanova Artigas's Faculty of Architecture and Urbanism, University of São Paulo, Brazil (1969), Schoeler & Heaton Architects' École Charlebois, Ottawa, Canada (1972), and Henning Larsen's Trondheim University, Norway (1978). Significant commercial atrium buildings before the 1970s include Alvar Aalto's Rautatalo Building, Helsinki, Finland (1955), and Eero Saarinen's Bell Laboratories, Holmdel, New Jersey (1962).

23. Compare Michael Osman's methodological approach to these issues in an earlier historical context in Michael Osman, *Modernism's Visible Hand: Architecture and Regulation in America* (Minneapolis: University of Minnesota Press, 2018).

Chapter 1

1. Previous studies of the atrium building have emphasized this kind of historical narrative. See Richard Saxon, *Atrium Buildings: Development and Design* (London: Architectural Press, 1983); Michael J. Bednar, *The New Atrium* (New York: McGraw-Hill, 1986). Saxon and Bednar point to a number of significant buildings, constructed through the nineteenth and early twentieth centuries, that featured atriums, including Sir Charles Barry's Reform Club, London (1841), Louis-Auguste Boileau's Le Bon Marché department store, Paris (1869), Montgomery Meigs's Pensions Building, Washington, D.C. (1887), Burnham & Root's Rookery Building, Chicago (1888), Frank Edbrooke's Brown Palace Hotel, Denver (1892), George Wyman's Bradbury Building, Los Angeles (1893), H. P. Berlage's Amsterdam Stock Exchange (1903), and Frank Lloyd Wright's Larkin Administration Building, Buffalo (1906). See Saxon, *Atrium Buildings*, 9–13; Bednar, *The New Atrium*, 5–31. The impetus for Johann Geist's encyclopedic study of arcades came from being a practicing architect designing an arcade in the 1970s. He noted a resurgence of interest in the type from the architectural profession at that time. See Johann Geist, *Arcades: The History of a Building Type*, trans. Jane O. Newman and John H. Smith (Cambridge, MA: MIT Press, 1983), vii.

2. Leslie Martin and Lionel March, "Land Use and Built Forms," *Cambridge Research* 3 (April 1966): 8.

3. The *Cambridge Research* article summarized findings from three research projects funded by the UK government to inform postwar urban development—the Offices Study, the Universities Study, and the Urban Systems Study—and enabled interconnected research on three distinct scales. See Dean Hawkes, "Bridging the Cultures: Architecture, Models and Computers in 1960s Cambridge," *Interdisciplinary Science Review* 42, nos. 1–2 (2017): 147. See also the contextual account given in Adam Sharr and Stephen Thornton, *Demolishing Whitehall: Leslie Martin, Harold Wilson and the Architecture of White Heat* (Farnham, Surrey: Ashgate, 2013), 169–198.

4. These parameters had underpinned building code provisions in the United Kingdom since the Second World War. See Dean Hawkes, "Building Bulk Legislation: A Description and Analysis," Working Paper no. 4, Centre for Land Use and Built Form Studies, University of Cambridge, n.d., 32–33. The paper was completed as part of the Offices Study.

5. Leslie Martin, *Whitehall: A Plan for the National and Government Centre* (London: Her Majesty's Stationery Office, 1965). Significantly, in their ziggurat-shaped section, the buildings would incorporate vast, top-lit galleries, likened in Martin's proposal to the Galleria Vittorio Emanuele II in Milan (Giuseppe Mengoni, 1877), creating a series of monumental "public interiors." Sharr and Thornton, *Demolishing Whitehall*, 101.

6. Hawkes, "Building Bulk Legislation," 9; emphasis in original.

7. Lionel March, Marcial Echeñique, and Peter Dickens, "Polemic for a Structural Revolution," *Architectural Design* 41 (May 1971): 275.

8. For an account of how the Centre was established and the work it undertook, see Lionel March, "'Setting Out the Possibilities': Leslie Martin and the Advancement of Architectural Knowledge," *Architectural Research Quarterly* 4, no. 4 (2000): 297–300; Hawkes, "Bridging the Cultures," 144–157; Sharr and Thornton, *Demolishing Whitehall*, 193; Sean Keller, *Automatic Architecture: Motivating Form after Modernism* (Chicago: University of Chicago Press, 2017), 39–43. The pavilion and court land use diagrams became the Centre's logo and that of its successor, the Martin Centre for Architectural and Urban Studies.

9. March, Echeñique, and Dickens, "Polemic for a Structural Revolution," 275.

10. Hawkes, "Building Bulk Legislation," 27–33. See also D. H. Crompton, "The Daylight Code: Some Notes on the Form of Control of Space about Buildings," *Town Planning Review* 26, no. 3 (October 1955): 155–164.

11. Hawkes, "Building Bulk Legislation," 20–22, 33–34. Martin and March defined the floor space index as "the gross floor area of a building measured outside the external walls divided by the site area including half the width of the surrounding roads. Plot ratio is the same gross measurement of floor area divided by the net site area. These measures are

expressed as 2:1, 3:1, etc." Martin and March, "Land Use and Built Forms," 9, n1. While they both refer to the same ratio, floor area ratio tends to be used in the United States, and plot ratio in the United Kingdom.

12. Crompton, "The Daylight Code," 155–164.

13. Hawkes, "Building Bulk Legislation," 23.

14. Hawkes, "Building Bulk Legislation," 40.

15. Hawkes, "Building Bulk Legislation," 41.

16. Hawkes, "Building Bulk Legislation," 41.

17. Martin and March, "Land Use and Built Forms," 9.

18. Martin and March, "Land Use and Built Forms," 8.

19. For each built form, Martin and March plotted what they called the "built potential" ("the ratio of the floor area of the built form to the site area") against the number of stories. For the pavilion form, above a certain point, an increase in stories showed a reduction in built potential, indicating a decrease in what they term "efficiency." Further, at the point that the pavilion form was at its maximum efficiency, the street and court forms displayed, respectively, two and three times the efficiency. Martin and March, "Land Use and Built Forms," 9, 11.

20. Martin and March, "Land Use and Built Forms," 11. It is telling that the authors also rejected the Corbusian "tower in the park" model on the basis that a desired "park" element would always be difficult to achieve given the infrastructure needed to service and facilitate the use of tall towers (8).

21. March, "'Setting Out the Possibilities,'" 299.

22. Martin and March, "Land Use and Built Forms," 13.

23. Lionel March, "Elementary Models of Built Forms," in *Urban Space and Structures*, ed. Leslie Martin and Lionel March (Cambridge: Cambridge University Press, 1972), 56. While the mathematical account of the built forms remained abstract, Martin had been influenced by Raymond Unwin's 1912 architectural study of density, *Nothing Gained by Overcrowding*. See the account in Dean Hawkes, "The Cambridge School: Tradition, Research, Practice," *Architectural Review* 175, no. 1047 (May 1984): 34.

24. For a background to the appearance and use of models in a range of disciplines at Cambridge at the time, see Lionel March, "Foreword," in *The Architecture of Form*, ed. Lionel March (Cambridge: Cambridge University Press, 1976), viii–ix; Hawkes, "Bridging the Cultures," 144–157.

25. March, "Elementary Models of Built Forms," 96.

26. March, "Foreword," vii.

27. Roger Scruton, "The Architecture of Stalinism," *Cambridge Review* 99 (26 November 1976): 36–41.

28. David Watkin, *Morality and Architecture: The Development of a Theme in Architectural History and Theory from the Gothic Revival to the Modern Movement* (Oxford: Clarendon Press, 1977), 12.

29. Keller, *Automatic Architecture*, 55–62. See also Mary-Louise Lobsinger, "Two Cambridges: Models, Methods, Systems and Expertise," in *A Second Modernism: MIT, Architecture, and the "Techno-Social" Moment*, ed. Arindam Dutta (Cambridge, MA: MIT Press, 2013), 652–685.

30. Philip Steadman, "Research in Architecture and Urban Studies at Cambridge in the 1960s and 1970s: What Really Happened," *Journal of Architecture* 21, no. 2 (2016): 291–306. Steadman studied at Cambridge under Martin and went straight into research upon graduation, becoming a founding member of LUBFS, and later the assistant director of the Martin Centre for Architectural and Urban Studies which absorbed LUBFS upon its establishment in 1974. Steadman also became a director of the spin-off company Applied Research of Cambridge, set up in 1969, which undertook work to commercialize research stemming from LUBFS, including the development of CAD systems, so that basic research and its practical application would be separated structurally.

31. See Mario Carpo, *The Second Digital Turn: Design beyond Intelligence* (Cambridge, MA: MIT Press, 2017); Molly Wright Steenson, *Architectural Intelligence: How Designers and Architects Created the Digital Landscape* (Cambridge, MA: MIT Press, 2017).

32. Alan Colquhoun, "Displacement of Concepts in Le Corbusier," in *Essays in Architectural Criticism: Modern Architecture and Historical Change* (Cambridge, MA: MIT Press, 1981), 66. First published in *Architectural Design* 43 (April 1972). See Keller's discussion of Colquhoun in relation to LUBFS in Keller, *Automatic Architecture*, 48–51.

33. Alan Colquhoun, "Typology and Design Method," in *Essays in Architectural Criticism*, 46. First published in *Arena* 83 (June 1967).

34. In a 1976 essay Dean Hawkes called upon a concept of stereotype to explain the pattern and development of solutions to distinct functional problems, his example being the postwar office building. See Dean Hawkes, "Type, Norms and Habit in Environmental Design," in March, *The Architecture of Form*, 465–481. His conception of stereotype was rooted in the evolution of form in relation to the kinds of parameters the LUBFS team was concerned with, that is, building controls and the environmental performance of different forms and their specific material and technological realization. For Hawkes, a stereotype was more akin to a paradigmatic building example than an abstract built form, yet one that was not deterministic in how its lessons could be understood and reapplied. While the development of stereotypes was in some senses progressive and "Darwinian," he argued

that their succession offered "a *store* of accumulated experience" that could be drawn on to develop different solutions to given problems, perhaps where "solutions with a high dependence on technology could co-exist with others which achieved their goals by simpler means" (481). In a later reflection on this theme, notably after the appearance of the atrium as an office building stereotype, he discussed the influence Colquhoun's essay "Typology and Design Method" had on his conception of stereotype. See Dean Hawkes, "Beyond the Environmental Tradition: Lessons from the Past for the Architecture of the Future," in *Interdisciplinary Design in Practice*, ed. Robin Spence, Sebastian Macmillan, and Paul Kirby (London: Institution of Civil Engineers, 2001), 159–169.

35. Colquhoun, "Typology and Design Method," 47.

36. Colquhoun, "Typology and Design Method," 47.

37. Colquhoun, "Typology and Design Method," 44.

38. Steadman, "Research in Architecture and Urban Studies at Cambridge," 297. He pointed to March's visual arts practice and his published scholarship on Frank Lloyd Wright and Rudolf Schindler, and the evidence of Martin's extensive body of built work, in particular his preoccupations with Scandinavian modernism (296–297).

39. Colquhoun, "Typology and Design Method," 47.

40. Aldo Rossi, *A Scientific Autobiography*, trans. Lawrence Venuti (Cambridge, MA: MIT Press, 1981); Aldo Rossi, *The Architecture of the City*, trans. Diane Ghirardo and Joan Ockman (Cambridge, MA: MIT Press, 1982).

41. Lawrence Barth, "The Complication of Type," in *Typological Formations: Renewable Building Types and the City*, ed. Christopher C. M. Lee and Sam Jacoby (London: AA Publications, 2007), 158.

42. *Collage City* should be seen in relation to the teaching and methods Rowe used in the Urban Design Studio at Cornell University, beginning in 1963. Figure-ground studies featured as an important technique of urban analysis and design, and several of the figure-ground studies published in *Collage City* were by Cornell students, significant among them being Wayne Copper, whose MArch thesis of 1967 consisted of a series of figure-ground drawings of historical cities. See the special issue on the studio: "Urban Design," *Cornell Journal of Architecture*, no. 2 (1982). The special issue featured a range of projects from the studio, and a discussion of the figure-ground technique in Wayne Copper, "The Figure/Grounds," *Cornell Journal of Architecture*, no. 2 (1982): 42–53.

43. Colin Rowe and Fred Koetter, *Collage City* (Cambridge, MA: MIT Press, 1978), 60.

44. Rowe and Koetter, *Collage City*, 62.

45. Rowe and Koetter, *Collage City*, 68.

46. Barth, "The Complication of Type," 164.

Chapter 2

1. John A. Sharry, "An Atrium Fire," *Fire Journal* 67, no. 6 (November 1973): 41. Another prominent atrium fire occurred at the International Monetary Fund (IMF) building in Washington, D.C., in 1977. See James K. Lathrop, "Atrium Fire Proves Difficult to Ventilate," *Fire Journal* 73, no. 1 (January 1979): 30–31. Both fires are discussed in George Atkinson, "Fire Hazards and the Design of Atria," *Building* 243, no. 41 (8 October 1982): 55; Alan Parnell and Gordon Butcher, "Smoke Control: Fire in Atria," *Building Services* 6, no. 6 (June 1984): 65–67; Anthony Ferguson, "Fire and the Atrium," *Architects' Journal* 181, no. 7 (13 February 1985): 63; and Richard Saxon, *Atrium Buildings: Development and Design* (London: Architectural Press, 1983), 94–95.

2. A contrary view was put forward by Richard Saxon. Writing in 1990 he argued: "Since the first modern atria in the US in 1967 over 1000 have been built. Only five fires have been recorded officially and all have been without loss of life." Richard Saxon, "Clearing the Smoke: Fire Safety in Atria," *Architects' Journal* 192, no. 10 (5 September 1990): 67.

3. See Portman's account of his "invention" of the atrium hotel in John Portman and Jonathan Barnett, *The Architect as Developer* (New York: McGraw-Hill, 1976), 28.

4. Gregory R. Miller, "Building Codes and Smoke Control," *Fire Safety Journal* 7, no. 1 (1984): 102.

5. Paul R. DeCicco, *Life Safety Considerations in Atrium Buildings* (Boston: Society of Fire Protection Engineers, 1982), 2.

6. John F. Behrens, "For Architects and Builders: Atriums," *Fire Journal* 75, no. 4 (July 1981): 6.

7. John G. Degenkolb, "Atriums," *Building Official and Code Administrator* 27, no. 6 (November/December 1983): 18.

8. DeCicco, *Life Safety Considerations in Atrium Buildings*, 9; Paul R. DeCicco et al., "Model Tests—Smoke Control Systems, N. Y. Portman Hotel," Polytechnic Institute of New York, 1975.

9. DeCicco, *Life Safety Considerations in Atrium Buildings*, 1.

10. G. O. Hansell and H. P. Morgan, "Fire Sizes and Sprinkler Effectiveness in Offices—Implications for Smoke Control Design," *Fire Safety Journal* 8, no. 3 (1984–1985): 187.

11. Liam Ross, "Regulatory Spaces, Physical and Metaphorical: On the Legal and Spatial Occupation of Fire-Safety Legislation," in *Industries of Architecture*, ed. Katie Lloyd Thomas, Tilo Amhoff, and Nick Beech (London: Routledge, 2016), 236.

12. Ross, "Regulatory Spaces, Physical and Metaphorical," 243. See also Ross's larger study of fire safety, regulation, and governmentality in which his previously published

work cited in this chapter is contained: Liam Ross, *Pyrotechnic Cities: Architecture, Fire Safety and Standardisation* (London: Routledge, 2022).

13. The Model Building Codes are the Building Officials and Code Administrators International (BOCA) Basic Building Code, the International Conference of Building Officials (ICBO) Uniform Building Code, the Southern Building Code Congress International (SBCCI) Standard Building Code, and the National Fire Protection Association (NFPA) Life Safety Code. The first three were used in different parts of the United States, with the NFPA code having national applicability. For a comparative analysis of these code provisions, see Miller, "Building Codes and Smoke Control," 99–106; and Michael J. Bednar, *The New Atrium* (New York: McGraw-Hill, 1986), 104–105. For the history of what are known as the model code groups, see David Listokin and David B. Hattis, "Building Codes and Housing," *Cityscape: A Journal of Policy Development and Research* 8, no. 1 (2005): 27.

14. Degenkolb, "Atriums," 18.

15. Degenkolb, "Atriums," 18. DeCicco noted that recent atriums varied vastly in their dimensions, suggesting that even a "threshold" definition of an atrium wouldn't describe its characteristics for the purposes of fire safety. DeCicco, *Life Safety Considerations in Atrium Buildings*, 2. In reflecting on the changes eventually made to the Model Building Codes, Miller defined the atrium via a convoluted series of negations. It is a definition that captures some sense of the confusion accompanying the codes' formulation. An atrium was thought to be "A structure wherein an opening through two or more floor levels exists other than enclosed stairways, elevator hoistways, escalators, plumbing, electrical, air conditioning or other equipment which is closed at the top and not defined as a mall." Miller, "Building Codes and Smoke Control," 100. This definition is cited by Michael Dillon, "Smoke Management System: Considerations for Hotel Atriums," *ASHRAE Journal* 25, no. 7 (July 1983): 46.

16. Wilton Berger, "Fire Safety in Atrium Buildings," *Buildings* [Chicago] 69, no. 4 (April 1975): 60. Berger had a plausible argument for the development of atriums from open courts, arguing that smoke and gases rise and then begin to cool, becoming heavier. In taller structures, this meant they could remain trapped within the court, staying within the structure without being cleared to the open air. He thought that atriums had become more prevalent because of the need to ventilate courts mechanically to mitigate this problem: ventilation would only become possible once a court became properly enclosed, that is, once it became an atrium. When it codified atrium spaces in its 1981 edition, the US National Fire Protection Association (NFPA) *Life Safety Code* would specify a minimum width of 20 feet, together with a minimum floor area of 1,000 feet. The 20-foot width accorded with the existing code for shopping malls. National Fire Protection Association, *Life Safety Code: Code for Safety to Life from Fire in Buildings and Structures,* NFPA no. 101 (Quincy, MA: National Fire Protection Association, 1981), section 6-2.2.3.1. See also the discussion in Behrens, "For Architects and Builders: Atriums," 6–7, 11.

17. Degenkolb, "Atriums," 18.

18. Portman and Barnett, *The Architect as Developer*, 19.

19. The Hyatt Regency Atlanta's foundational status is acknowledged in fire safety articles including Rolf Jensen, "Fire Protection for Hotels and Other Leisure Centers," *Actual Specifying Engineer* 31, no. 2 (February 1974): 112; DeCicco, *Life Safety Considerations in Atrium Buildings*, 2; and Degenkolb, "Atriums," 18.

20. Charles Rice, *Interior Urbanism: Architecture, John Portman and Downtown America* (London: Bloomsbury, 2016), 31–62.

21. E. G. Butcher and A. C. Parnell, "Atrium Buildings: A Discussion Using Overseas Information," *Fire Surveyor* 11, no. 5 (October 1982): 44; emphasis in original.

22. See Saxon, *Atrium Buildings*, 93.

23. A. C. Parnell, "Atrium Buildings and Fire Safety," *Fire Surveyor* 8, no. 5 (October 1979): 37–39.

24. Degenkolb, "Atriums," 21.

25. Degenkolb, "Atriums," 22. See also DeCicco, *Life Safety Considerations in Atrium Buildings*, 5.

26. DeCicco, *Life Safety Considerations in Atrium Buildings*, 5.

27. Miller, "Building Codes and Smoke Control," 105.

28. Butcher and Parnell, "Atrium Buildings: A Discussion Using Overseas Information," 47. Their book, *Smoke Control in Fire Safety Design* (London: E. & F.N. Spon, 1979), was used as a reference by the BOCA committee. See Degenkolb, "Atriums," 19.

29. Butcher and Parnell, "Atrium Buildings: A Discussion Using Overseas Information," 46–47. Their theory was partly borne out by the experience of the IMF fire. See also Lathrop, "Atrium Fire Proves Difficult to Ventilate," 30–31.

30. Building Officials and Code Administrators International, *The BOCA Basic Building Code/1981*, 8th ed. (Chicago: Building Officials and Code Administrators International, 1981), section 631.2.1.5.

31. On the question of equivalency, see Behrens, "For Architects and Builders: Atriums," 6. The National Fire Protection Association's *Life Safety Code: Code for Safety to Life from Fire in Buildings and Structures* (1981) was explicit about its equivalency provisions at the beginning of the code document: "Nothing in this *Code* is intended to prevent the use of systems, methods, or devices of equivalent or superior quality, strength, fire resistance, effectiveness, durability, and safety to those prescribed by this *Code*, providing technical documentation is submitted to the authority having jurisdiction to demonstrate equivalency and the system, method, or device is approved for the intended purpose." National Fire Protection Association, *Life Safety Code*, 101-3 (section 1-5.1).

32. Jensen, "Fire Protection for Hotels and Other Leisure Centers," 112–113.

33. Jensen, "Fire Protection for Hotels and Other Leisure Centers," 112.

34. Donald Boehmer, "Fire Protection System for an Atrium Satisfies Code Intent," *Architectural Record* 158, no. 5 (October 1975): 125–128.

35. Behrens, "For Architects and Builders: Atriums," 6.

36. Vincent Brannigan, "Fire Scenarios or Scenario Fires? Can Fire Safety Science Provide the Critical Inputs for Performance-Based Fire Safety Analyses?," *Fire Safety Science* 6 (2000): 207–218. See the discussion of Brannigan's argument in Ross, "Regulatory Spaces, Physical and Metaphorical," 241–243.

37. Brannigan, "Fire Scenarios or Scenario Fires?," 210.

38. Brannigan, "Fire Scenarios or Scenario Fires?," 212.

39. Brannigan, "Fire Scenarios or Scenario Fires?," 211.

40. Milosh Puchovsky, "NFPA's Perspectives on Performance-Based Codes and Standards," *Fire Technology* 32 (November 1996): 325. See the international overview of performance-based code development in Brian Meacham, "International Development and Use of Performance-Based Building Codes and Fire Safety Design Methods," *SFPE Bulletin* (March/April 1995): 7–16. See also J. Kenneth Richardson, "Changing the Regulatory System to Accept Fire Safety Engineering Methods," *Journal of Fire Protection Engineering* 5, no. 4 (November 1993): 135–140; J. Kenneth Richardson, "Moving towards Performance-Based Codes," *NFPA Journal* (May/June 1994): 70–78.

41. Puchovsky, "NFPA's Perspectives on Performance-Based Codes and Standards," 329.

42. Brannigan, "Fire Scenarios or Scenario Fires?," 214. See also Liam Ross, "Creative Uncertainty: Arup Associates, Fire Safety, and the Metaengineering of Government," in *Neoliberalism on the Ground: Architecture and Transformation from the 1960s to the Present*, ed. Kenny Cupers, Catharina Gabrielsson, and Helena Mattsson (Pittsburgh: University of Pittsburgh Press, 2020), 280–281; Ross, "Regulatory Spaces, Physical and Metaphorical," 242.

43. Ferguson, "Fire and the Atrium," 63.

44. Ferguson, "Fire and the Atrium," 63. In addition, the GLC memo explicitly rejected mechanical ventilation of an atrium, though it did stipulate sprinklering of glazed surfaces facing the atrium to prevent the spread of fire between floors. See also Parnell and Butcher, "Smoke Control: Fire in Atria," 65.

45. The first atrium hotel in London was the Sheraton Skyline at Heathrow Airport by Ronald Fielding with Curtis & Davis (1971).

46. Greater London Council, *Fire Safety for the Atrium: Technical Information Note* (London: Greater London Council, 1985). This guidance did specify mechanical smoke extraction.

47. Ferguson, "Fire and the Atrium," 69.

48. Saxon, "Clearing the Smoke," 65.

49. See the account of Amy Thomas, "The Political Economy of Flexibility: Deregulation and the Transformation of Corporate Space in the Postwar City of London," in Cupers, Gabrielsson, and Mattsson, *Neoliberalism on the Ground*, 142–143. There was some tension and discrepancy between the approach of the ARCUK and that of the RIBA in revising their codes of conduct. See Denise Searle, "The New Morality," *Building Design* 530 (30 January 1981): 7; Neal Morris, "RIBA Reminds All Members about Fixed Fee Scale," *Building Design* 551 (26 June 1981): 3. In 1978 the American Institute of Architects (AIA) began moves to change their code of ethical and professional conduct in large part driven by litigation from the US Department of Justice for possible violations of antitrust laws. A new, voluntary statement of ethical principles was adopted in 1980. See "Convention Votes to Discard AIA Mandatory Code of Ethics," *AIA Journal* 69, no. 8 (July 1980): 11, 14. See the discussion in Jay Wickersham, "From Disinterested Expert to Marketplace Competitor: How Anti-Monopoly Law Transformed the Ethics and Economics of American Architecture in the 1970s," *Architectural Theory Review* 20, no. 2 (2015): 138–158.

50. See Listokin and Hattis, "Building Codes and Housing," 27. For a comparative discussion of US and UK deregulation, including the politicization of changes to local government in the United Kingdom, see Robin Hambleton, "Urban Government under Thatcher and Reagan," Institute of Urban and Regional Development, University of California, Berkeley, Working Paper no. 484 (July 1988).

51. Secretary of State for the Environment and Secretary of State for Wales, *The Future of Building Control in England and Wales*, Cmnd. 8179 (London: Her Majesty's Stationery Office, 1981), 4.

52. See the discussion in Margaret Law, "Fire Safety Design Practices in the UK—New Building Regulations," *Conference on Fire Safety Design in the 21st Century*, Worcester, MA, 8–10 May 1991; republished in *Engineering Fire Safety: Some Selected Papers by Margaret Law* (London: Arup, 2002), 240–248. However, at the time Law was writing, there was still no established pathway to accredit fire safety engineers as approved inspectors.

53. Department of the Environment, *Streamlining the Cities: Government Proposals for Reorganising Local Government in Greater London and the Metropolitan Counties*, Cmnd. 9063 (London: Her Majesty's Stationery Office, 1983).

54. The GLC leader at the time was Labour politician Ken Livingstone, who decried its abolition as entirely politically motivated. See Ken Livingstone, "Confound Their Politics!," *Town and Country Planning* 52, no. 12 (December 1983): 335. Livingstone became Mayor of London under a newly constituted Greater London Authority in 2000, serving until 2008. For a detailed examination of the effects of the dissolution of the GLC,

see Tony Travers, "London after Abolition," *Local Government Studies* 16, no. 3 (1990): 105–116.

55. Alan Porter, "Recent Developments in Atrium Buildings," *Architect and Surveyor* 64, no. 11 (December 1989): 15.

56. Ferguson, "Fire and the Atrium," 69.

57. London District Surveyors Association, *Fire Safety in Atrium Buildings*, Fire Safety Guide no. 2 (London: London District Surveyors Association, 1989); British Standards Institution, *Draft BS for Fire Precautions in the Design, Construction and Use of Buildings: Part 7. Code of Practice for Atrium Buildings* (London: British Standards Institution, 1990); Loss Prevention Council, *REC RC 21 Recommendations for the Fire Protection of Atrium Buildings* (London: Loss Prevention Council, 1990). For a discussion of the LSDA code, see Saxon, "Clearing the Smoke," 65, 67. In this article Saxon noted the imminent arrival of the British Standards Institution code, which was being "written by Warrington Fire Research, Building Design Partnership (BDP) and Rolf Jensen (author of some US codes)" (65). As well as the author of several books on atriums, Saxon was a partner in Building Design Partnership; Alan Porter was part of Warrington Fire Research, and Rolf Jensen published one of the earliest discussions of smoke control in atriums in the United States. See Saxon's discussion of the British Standards Institution code in Richard Saxon, "Keeping Smoke at Bay: Atria, Malls, Galleria," *Architects' Journal* 193, no. 9 (27 February 1991): 46, and for his discussion of this code and the Loss Prevention Council's code, see Saxon, *The Atrium Comes of Age* (Harlow: Longman, 1994), 84–93. By 1990, all the relevant US codes that had first included reference to atriums around 1980 had been further updated.

58. George Atkinson, "New Science Master for London," *Building* 247, no. 32 (10 August 1984): 47–49.

59. George Atkinson, "If the GLC Goes, Will Standards Drop?," *Building* 248, no. 11 (15 March 1985): 90.

60. R. E. H. Read, *A Short History of the Fire Research Station, Borehamwood* (Watford: Building Research Establishment, 1994), xii. Ross dates the establishment of the Fire Research Station to 1949. Ross, "Creative Uncertainty," 273.

61. H. P. Morgan, *Smoke Control Methods in Enclosed Shopping Complexes of One or More Stories, a Design Summary* (London: Her Majesty's Stationery Office, 1979). The enclosed shopping center remained the reference point for discussions about atriums in the United Kingdom; however, the guidance was limited to structures of two stories. See Atkinson, "Fire Hazards and the Design of Atria," 57. Updated guidance on shopping malls was published in 1990 and extended to multistory malls: H. P. Morgan and J. P. Gardner, *Design Principles for Smoke Ventilation in Enclosed Shopping Centres* (Borehamwood: Building Research Establishment, 1990).

62. Hansell and Morgan, "Fire Sizes and Sprinkler Effectiveness in Offices," 187–198. See also the exchange of letters between these two authors and Margaret Law regarding methodological issues and the development of the research program. M. Law, "Comments on 'Fire Sizes and Sprinkler Effectiveness in Offices—Implications for Smoke Control Design,'" *Fire Safety Journal* 10, no. 1 (1986): 67–68; G. O. Hansell and H. P. Morgan, "Reply to Comments on 'Fire Sizes and Sprinkler Effectiveness in Offices—Implications for Smoke Control Design,'" *Fire Safety Journal* 10, no. 1 (1986): 69–70.

63. G. O. Hansell and H. P. Morgan, "Atrium Buildings: Calculating Smoke Flows in Atria for Smoke-Control Design," *Fire Safety Journal* 12, no. 1 (February 1987): 10. This paper was also the subject of an exchange of letters with Law: Margaret Law, "Comments on 'Atrium Buildings: Calculating Smoke Flows in Atria for Smoke-control Design,'" *Fire Safety Journal* 13, no. 2–3 (1988): 219; G. O. Hansell and H. P. Morgan, "Atrium Building Smoke Flows," *Fire Safety Journal* 13, no. 2–3 (1988): 221–224.

64. Hansell and Morgan, "Atrium Buildings: Calculating Smoke Flows in Atria for Smoke-Control Design," 11. The pair would author a further two-part paper: G. O. Hansell, and H. P. Morgan, "Smoke Control in Atrium Buildings Using Depressurisation, Part 1: Design Principles," *Fire Science and Technology* 10, no. 1–2 (1990): 11–26; G. O. Hansell, and H. P. Morgan, "Smoke Control in Atrium Buildings Using Depressurisation, Part 2: Considerations Affecting Practical Design," *Fire Science and Technology* 10, no. 1–2 (1990): 27–41.

65. A paper authored solely by Hansell was intended for building control officers. Graham Hansell, "Smoke Control in Atrium Buildings," *Building Control*, no. 22 (May/June 1987): 40–51.

66. G. O. Hansell and H. P. Morgan, *Design Approaches for Smoke Control in Atrium Buildings* (Borehamwood: Building Research Establishment, 1994).

67. Margaret Law, "The Value of Fire Research," *Architects' Journal* 176, no. 36 (8 September 1982): 77–78; Atkinson, "Fire Hazards and the Design of Atria," 57.

68. Corinne Williams, Howard Morgan, and Earle Perera, "Coping with Smoke in Atria," *Architects' Journal* 209, no. 3 (21 January 1999): 37–39.

69. S. Peacock and R. Frost, "Active Protection for Atria," *Building Services* 13, no. 9 (September 1991): 32–35.

70. Barrie Evans, "Controlling Air Flow to Fight Fire," *Architects' Journal* 204, no. 17 (7 November 1996): 44. On the relationship between research, consultancy, and architectural services under deregulation, see Amy Thomas, "Architectural Consulting in the Knowledge Economy: DEGW and the Orbit Report," *Journal of Architecture* 24, no. 7 (2019): 1020–1044.

71. Evans, "Controlling Air Flow to Fight Fire," 44. See, for example, the discussion of code changes by the mid-2000s in the United States regarding atriums in Jeffrey S. Tubbs,

"Smoke Management in the 2006 IBC," *ASHRAE Journal* 48, no. 10 (October 2006): 50–55.

72. Ross, "Regulatory Spaces, Physical and Metaphorical," 242.

73. Ross, "Creative Uncertainty," 274–277.

74. Dean Hawkes, "Air Apparent," *Architects' Journal* 178, no. 31 (3 August 1983): 26–34. See also "Gateway 2," *Arup Journal* 19, no. 2 (June 1984): 2–9.

75. Ross, "Creative Uncertainty," 271.

76. Ross, "Creative Uncertainty," 277–278. See also the discussion in R. A. Waters, "Stansted Terminal Building and Early Atrium Studies," *Journal of Fire Protection Engineering* 1, no. 2 (1989): 63–76.

77. Amy Thomas, "Risk in 'the Room': Negotiating New Economic Paradigms in the Architecture of Lloyd's of London Insurance Market," *Architectural Theory Review* 26, no. 1 (2022): 7–34. See also Jonathan Massey, "Risk Design," *Grey Room* 54 (Winter 2014): 6–33, for a discussion of Swiss Re's London headquarters, 30 St. Mary Axe, by Foster + Partners (2004). Massey deploys the concept of a "risk imaginary" to discuss the way in which the spatial and technical aspects of the building's design mediate perceptions of risk.

78. Ross, "Creative Uncertainty," 278–280. On what he calls Arup's practice of "metaengineering," see Arindam Dutta, "Marginality and Metaengineering: Keynes and Arup," in *Governing by Design: Architecture, Economy, and Politics in the Twentieth Century*, ed. Aggregate Architectural History Collaborative (Pittsburgh: University of Pittsburgh Press, 2012), 237–267.

79. See the discussion of the project in Charles Rice, "Fast Building: Money, Management and Risk at London's Chelsea Harbour Development," *Architectural Theory Review* 26, no. 1 (2022): 56–75.

80. Brian Finnimore, "The Need for Atria Fire Codes," *Fire Prevention* 205 (December 1987): 30.

81. Colin Davies, "Building Up Speed," *Architects' Journal* 178, no. 27 (6 July 1983): 28.

Chapter 3

1. Dean Hawkes and Richard MacCormac, "Office Form, Energy and Land Use," *RIBA Journal* 85, no. 6 (June 1978): 246. The article was part of a special issue on "Energy and Built Form."

2. Dean Hawkes, "Atria and Conservatories 1: Introduction and Case Study 1," *Architects' Journal* 177, no. 19 (11 May 1983): 68.

3. Hawkes, "Atria and Conservatories 1," 67.

4. Michelle Murphy, *Sick Building Syndrome and the Problem of Uncertainty: Environmental Politics, Technoscience, and Women Workers* (Durham: Duke University Press, 2006), 6.

5. Gail Cooper, *Air-Conditioning America: Engineers and the Controlled Environment, 1900–1960* (Baltimore: Johns Hopkins University Press, 1998), 7.

6. Murphy, *Sick Building Syndrome*, 20.

7. Cooper, *Air-Conditioning America*, 69–71.

8. Cooper, *Air-Conditioning America*, 73.

9. Cooper, *Air-Conditioning America*, 75.

10. Murphy, *Sick Building Syndrome*, 23.

11. Daniel A. Barber, *Modern Architecture and Climate: Design before Air Conditioning* (Princeton: Princeton University Press, 2020), 246.

12. Murphy, *Sick Building Syndrome*, 28.

13. P. O. Fanger, *Thermal Comfort: Analysis and Applications in Environmental Engineering* (New York: McGraw-Hill, 1970), 41–42, 110–128. PMV was supplemented by an equation that determined the "predicted percentage of dissatisfied," or PPD, which, for Fanger, was "simply an expression for the number of 'potential complainers'" (128). See also the discussion in D. A. McIntyre, *Indoor Climate* (London: Applied Science Publishers, 1980), 176–183.

14. For a critique of Fanger's methods and their impact on standards, see Elizabeth Shove, *Comfort, Cleanliness and Convenience* (Oxford: Berg, 2003), 31–33.

15. Fanger, *Thermal Comfort*, 14.

16. D. J. Fisk noted that Fanger's equation and the resulting idea of the comfort of a sedentary subject did not consider exterior climate, ethnicity, time of day, age, sex, or body build. D. J. Fisk, *Thermal Control of Buildings* (London: Applied Science Publishers, 1981), 18. Fanger called these "special factors," positing that "most of these factors have little or no effect upon the comfort conditions, and the comfort equation can therefore be used without modifications in the majority of cases in practice." Fanger, *Thermal Comfort*, 43.

17. Murphy, *Sick Building Syndrome*, 25.

18. Murphy, *Sick Building Syndrome*, 20–27.

19. Barber, *Modern Architecture and Climate*, 10. For a discussion of how ASHRAE standards underpinned the uptake of air-conditioned buildings in tropical climates, see Jiat-Hwee Chang, *A Genealogy of Tropical Architecture: Colonial Networks, Nature and Technoscience* (London: Routledge, 2016), 248, 251. See also Jiat-Hwee Chang, "Thermal Comfort and Climatic Design in the Tropics: An Historical Critique," *Journal of Architecture* 21, no. 8 (December 2016): 1172–1202.

20. Joseph M. Siry, *Air-Conditioning in Modern American Architecture, 1890–1970* (University Park: Pennsylvania State University Press, 2022), 159. Siry analyzes in detail the use of air-conditioning in a range of midcentury office buildings in the United States (159–192).

21. Beat Meyer, *Indoor Air Quality* (Reading, MA: Addison-Wesley, 1983), 324. Meyer understood this to be an effect of a developer-driven model of building procurement, where "builder, owner, and occupant are often three different parties," meaning that the "separation between capital and operating costs is not conducive to energy-efficient design, and indoor air quality. In the early sixties, many large office buildings were built without light switches and without provisions for reduced nighttime and weekend heating or ventilation" (80).

22. Meyer, *Indoor Air Quality*, 7.

23. Richard G. Stein, "Observations on Energy Use in Buildings," *Journal of Architectural Education* 30, no. 3 (February 1977): 36. See also Philip Oldfield, Dario Trabucco, and Antony Wood, "Five Energy Generations of Tall Buildings: An Historical Analysis of Energy Consumption in High-Rise Buildings," *Journal of Architecture* 14, no. 5 (September 2009): 599.

24. Meyer, *Indoor Air Quality*, 8, 66, 315–316. This was ASHRAE Standard 62-1981, "Ventilation for Acceptable Indoor Air Quality."

25. Meyer, *Indoor Air Quality*, 69. This was ANSI-ASHRAE-TIES Standard 90-1980, "Energy Conservation in New Building Design."

26. Meyer, *Indoor Air Quality*, 293, 325.

27. Meyer, *Indoor Air Quality*, 62.

28. Meyer, *Indoor Air Quality*, 69, 87. Other safety risks were also identified relative to retrofitting insulation, including increased risk of fire. See Gordon Butcher and Alan Parnell, "Too Hot for Comfort," *Building* 235, no. 49 (8 December 1978): 85–86.

29. Meyer, *Indoor Air Quality*, 7. See also Tom Fisher and Fred S. Dubin, "Up in the Air," *Progressive Architecture* 64, no. 4 (April 1983): 106.

30. Meyer, *Indoor Air Quality*, 7–9; Murphy, *Sick Building Syndrome*, 82–83.

31. Hal Levin and Kevin Teichman, "Indoor Air Quality—For Architects," *Progressive Architecture* 72, no. 3 (March 1991): 52. See also J. M. Sykes, "Sick Building Syndrome," *Building Services Engineering Research and Technology* 10, no. 1 (1989): 1–11; Murphy, *Sick Building Syndrome*, 108–109.

32. Meyer, *Indoor Air Quality*, 66. See the discussion in Michael R. Greenberg, "Indoor Air Quality: Protecting Public Health through Design, Planning, and Research," *Journal of Architectural and Planning Research* 3, no. 3 (August 1986): 254–256; Fisher and Dubin,

"Up in the Air," 106; James B. Gardner, "Cleaning Indoor Air," *Interior Design* 58, no. 11 (September 1987): 293. In the United Kingdom, the Chartered Institution of Building Services Engineers (CIBSE), played a similar role to ASHRAE in the United States. They provided guidance on ventilation and indoor air quality standards, and the British Standards Institution also published codes of practice for ventilation. These had the status of approved documents relative to UK building legislation. See John Harrison, Anthony Pickering, and A. J. Wilson, "Risks and Remedies. Indoor Air Quality: 1. The Risks," *Architects' Journal* 185, no. 23 (10 June 1987): 57–59.

33. Meyer, *Indoor Air Quality*, 13. See also Fisher and Dubin, "Up in the Air," 106.

34. Alan Field, "The Sick Building Syndrome," *Building Services* 6, no. 11 (November 1984): 39.

35. See Murphy, *Sick Building Syndrome*, 92–95.

36. Murphy's account revolves around the issue of the "reality" of sick building syndrome, and the way in which "an expert or lay tradition made chemical exposures perceptible or imperceptible, existent or non-existent." Murphy, *Sick Building Syndrome*, 7.

37. Field, "The Sick Building Syndrome," 39.

38. Field, "The Sick Building Syndrome," 40.

39. Sykes, "Sick Building Syndrome," 3.

40. Greenberg, "Indoor Air Quality," 259. See also Fisher and Dubin, "Up in the Air," 108.

41. Greenberg, "Indoor Air Quality," 255.

42. Greenberg, "Indoor Air Quality," 256.

43. Murphy, *Sick Building Syndrome*, 82–83, 145–148.

44. Murphy, *Sick Building Syndrome*, 34.

45. Murphy, *Sick Building Syndrome*, 57–80.

46. Murphy, *Sick Building Syndrome*, 32. Research into the ability of houseplants to remove chemicals from sealed environments was commissioned by the National Aeronautics and Space Administration together with the Associated Landscape Contractors of America, underlining the continued primacy of the artificial environment in research efforts and the commercial opportunities it provided. See Penny Sparke, *Nature Inside: Plants and Flowers in the Modern Interior* (New Haven: Yale University Press, 2020), 178.

47. Greenberg, "Indoor Air Quality," 259–260. See also Fisher and Dubin, "Up in the Air," 106; Gardner, "Cleaning Indoor Air," 292–293. Two articles in the *Architects' Journal* framed the "state of the art" on indoor air quality for architects, drawing on current research in the health sciences: Harrison, Pickering, and Wilson, "Risks and Remedies.

Indoor Air Quality: 1. The Risks"; Peter Warren, A. J. Wilson, and Richard Rooley, "Risks and Remedies. Indoor Air Quality: 2. The Remedies," *Architects' Journal* 185, no. 24 (17 June 1987): 57–63.

48. As Frank A. Mills noted, the fact that users "enjoy the advantages of additional 'indoor' space with 'external' qualities is an acknowledged phenomenon that is attracting interest from researchers involved in the study of building uses and health issues such as sick building syndrome." Frank A. Mills, "Energy-Efficient Commercial Atrium Buildings," *ASHRAE Transactions* 100, part 1 (1994): 667.

49. Dean Hawkes, "Building Shape and Energy Use," in *The Architecture of Energy*, ed. Dean Hawkes and Janet Owers (London: Construction Press, 1981), 24.

50. Hawkes, "Building Shape and Energy Use," 25.

51. Reyner Banham, *The Architecture of the Well-Tempered Environment* (London: Architectural Press, 1969).

52. Hawkes, "Building Shape and Energy Use," 25.

53. Hawkes, "Building Shape and Energy Use," 28.

54. "Hotel Envelops a Cavernous Courtyard," *Engineering News-Record* (29 July 1965): 27.

55. Greenberg would go on to form an architectural partnership with Dean Hawkes.

56. On the internalized environment of the Willis Faber & Dumas Headquarters, see Alexandra Quantrill, "Parcel, Bubble, Shell: The Insular Environment of Finance," *Architectural Theory Review* 26, no. 1 (2022): 195–212.

57. Gordon had undertaken research on the energy efficiency of three office building designs with deep-plan arrangements. One was naturally ventilated and contained open courts, and the other two, one of which was his design for the Crown Offices, contained covered internal courts and were air-conditioned. In establishing the energy credentials of air-conditioned buildings with covered courts, his research orientation was perhaps the opposite of Hawkes and MacCormac, who pursued the efficiency of the covered court for naturally ventilated designs. While not directly comparable, Gordon found that air-conditioned deep-plan buildings could be as energy-efficient as naturally ventilated ones if lighting levels were maintained at reasonable levels. See Alex Gordon, "Future Office Design: Energy Implications," *Journal of Architectural Research* 3, no. 3 (September 1974): 6–14.

58. George Kasabov, "Technics, Necessity and Choice," in Hawkes and Owers, *The Architecture of Energy*, 247. Kasabov, together with the RIBA Energy Group, had organized a conference and exhibition at the RIBA in 1976 as the centerpiece of the Institute's efforts in energy conservation which had begun in 1972 under then-President Alex Gordon. See George Kasabov, ed., *Buildings: The Key to Energy Conservation. Issues and Case Studies* (London: RIBA Energy Group, 1979).

59. Max Fordham, "A Participant's Reflection on the Conference," in Hawkes and Owers, *The Architecture of Energy*, 231.

60. Lionel March, "Elementary Models of Built Forms," in *Urban Space and Structures*, ed. Leslie Martin and Lionel March (Cambridge: Cambridge University Press, 1972), 56.

61. See the way in which his account of the "Architecture of Energy" was presented in terms of glass architecture in Dean Hawkes, "Glass and the Architecture of Energy," *RIBA Journal* 88, no. 2 (February 1981): 50–52.

62. Hawkes, "Atria and Conservatories 1," 68; Nick Baker, "Atria and Conservatories 2: Case Study 2," *Architects' Journal* 177, no. 20 (18 May 1983): 67–69; Nick Baker, "Atria and Conservatories 3: Principles of Design," *Architects' Journal* 177, no. 21 (25 May 1983): 67–70.

63. Dean Hawkes, "Vault Face," *Architects' Journal* 177, no. 19 (11 May 1983): 59.

64. Hawkes, "Vault Face," 59.

65. Dean Hawkes, "Air Apparent," *Architects' Journal* 178, no. 31 (3 August 1983): 30.

66. Hawkes, "Air Apparent," 30.

67. Hawkes, "Air Apparent," 34.

68. Dean Hawkes, "Energy Revisit: Gateway Two," *Architects' Journal* 180, no. 46 (14 November 1984): 73.

69. Hawkes, "Energy Revisit: Gateway Two," 72.

70. Fisk, *Thermal Control of Buildings*.

71. D. J. Fisk, "Comfort and Energy Consumption," in Hawkes and Owers, *The Architecture of Energy*, 35. These ideas were broadly echoed by another contributor, John Berry from Arup, who posited: "The so-called 'normal' environmental specification for commercial buildings is unnecessarily rigid and limits the scope for energy conservation, particularly in terms of built form." John Berry, "Control of the Built Environment: Its Impact in Energy Conservation," in Hawkes and Owers, *The Architecture of Energy*, 84.

72. Nick Baker, "The Irritable Occupant: Recent Developments in Thermal Comfort Theory," *Architectural Research Quarterly* 2, no. 2 (Winter 1996): 84–90. Accepting that his PMV model had been developed in relation to air-conditioned buildings and acknowledging the existence of adaptive strategies used by occupants to manage their thermal comfort, particularly in non-air-conditioned buildings in warmer climates, Fanger has sought to develop a calculable extension to his PMV model to account for larger variances in acceptable levels of comfort. P. Ole Fanger and Jørn Toftum, "Extension of the PMV Model to Non-Air-Conditioned Buildings in Warm Climates," *Energy and Buildings* 34, no. 6 (July 2002): 533–536.

73. David Morton, "Children's Hospital of Philadelphia: Chopping Energy Costs," *Progressive Architecture* 56, no. 5 (May 1975): 46–53.

74. Steve Steinberg, "Warehouse Conjures Savings Out of Air," *Building Design and Construction* 22 (October 1981): 43–47.

75. "Office Blocks with Stacked Atriums Save Owners Construction and Energy Costs," *Architectural Record* 169, no. 15 (November 1981): 120–127.

76. James B. Gardner, "Daylighting Cuts Energy Use to 19,600 BTU per sq ft per year," *Architectural Record* 172, no. 1 (January 1984): 138–143.

77. Allan Temko, "California's New Generation of Energy Efficient State Buildings," *AIA Journal* 66, no. 13 (December 1977): 50–56. For an analysis of the California State Office Building program, see Sam Davis, *Designing for Energy Efficiency: A Study of Eight California State Office Buildings*, Department of Architecture, University of California, Berkeley, 1981. Interestingly, the Bateson Building had suffered from the effects of sick building syndrome, mostly due to offgassing from new carpets and furniture installations and defective HVAC components. The effects were able to be mitigated, however, due to the building's ability to be naturally ventilated. See "Air Quality Problems Plague California State Building," *AIA Journal* 71, no. 11 (September 1982): 18, 22. See also Simon Sadler, "The Bateson Building, Sacramento, California, 1977–81, and the Design of a New Age State," *Journal of the Society of Architectural Historians* 75, no. 4 (December 2016): 469–489.

78. "Engineered Daylighting for an Energy Company in Houston," *Architectural Record* 166, no. 3 (August 1979): 102–105.

79. Scott Matthews and Peter Calthorpe, "Daylight as a Central Determinant of Design," *AIA Journal* 68, no. 11 (September 1979): 86–93. Calthorpe was also a designer, with Van der Ryn, of the Bateson Building. See Temko, "California's New Generation of Energy Efficient State Buildings," 52.

80. Jim Murphy, "SERI Headquarters, Golden, Co.: Solar Nexus," *Progressive Architecture* 61, no. 4 (April 1980): 126–129.

81. Suzanne Stephens, "Going Solar in the City," *Progressive Architecture* 61, no. 4 (April 1980): 113–116. For a history of urban shade in Los Angeles, see Sam Bloch, "Shade," *Places Journal*, April 2019, accessed 12 May 2022, https://doi.org/10.22269/190423

82. Donald Watson, "The Energy within the Space Within," *Progressive Architecture* 63, no. 7 (July 1982): 97–102.

83. Buford W. Duke Jr., "Energy Performance in Atriums—An Affirmation," *ASHRAE Journal* 25, no. 7 (July 1983): 34–39; Buford W. Duke Jr., "The Practical Case for Atriums," *ASHRAE Transactions* 89, no. 2B (1983): 797–811.

84. Boggarm S. V. Setty, "Atriums: The HVAC Factor," *ASHRAE Journal* 25, no. 7 (July 1983): 40–45.

85. For a discussion of these strategies see Mills, "Energy-Efficient Commercial Atrium Buildings," 665–675.

86. Mills, "Energy-Efficient Commercial Atrium Buildings," 665. See also Mills's attempts to summarize and codify the main environmental performance characteristics of atriums in Frank Mills, "Environmental Design of Atrium Buildings in the UK," *ASHRAE Transactions* 96, part 1 (1990): 14–22.

87. Ida Bryn, "Atrium Buildings Environmental Design and Energy Use," *ASHRAE Transactions* 99, part 1 (1993): 1082–1091. The broader program findings, including the atrium studies, were published as A. Hildon and A. Seager, eds., *Passive and Hybrid Solar Commercial Buildings: Basic Case Studies* (Harwell, Oxfordshire: Energy Technology Support Unit, Harwell Laboratory, 1989), and S. R. Hastings, ed., *Passive Solar Commercial and Institutional Buildings: A Sourcebook of Examples and Design Insights* (Chichester: John Wiley & Sons, 1994). See also the report on the overall project in Robert J. Hitchcock, Mary-Margaret Jenior, and William L. Carroll, "Energy-Efficient Atriums," *Urban Land* 51, no. 12 (December 1992): 28–32.

88. A. Seager, "Gateway Two, Basingstoke. EPA Non-domestic Technical Report," ETSU Report 1160/11, 1992.

89. Mills, "Energy-Efficient Commercial Atrium Buildings," 669.

90. A. Sluce et al., "Passive Solar Design Studies of Non-domestic Buildings. Phase II: Atrium Design Studies," Design Reports. ETSU S/N1/00081/REP/B, 1993, 2. See also A. Seager, ed. *Passive and Hybrid Solar Commercial Buildings: Advanced Case Studies Seminar* (Harwell, Oxfordshire: Energy Technology Support Unit, Harwell Laboratory, 1991).

91. Sluce et al., "Passive Solar Design Studies of Non-domestic Buildings," 2.

92. J. R. Stammers, *Atrium Buildings: Numbers and Future Trends* (Harwell, Oxfordshire: Energy Technology Support Unit, Harwell Laboratory, 1994).

93. Dean Hawkes, *An Architect's Guide to the General Principles of Energy-Conscious Atrium Building Design* (Harwell, Oxfordshire: Energy Technology Support Unit, Harwell Laboratory, 1994).

94. Nick Baker and Koen Steemers, *The LT Method 2.0: An Energy Design Tool for Non-Domestic Buildings* (Cambridge: Cambridge Architectural Research, 1995); see the application of this method specifically for atrium buildings in Dennis Ho, "Climatic Responsive Atrium Design in Europe," *Architectural Research Quarterly* 1, no. 1 (Spring 1996): 64–75.

95. N. Baker, A. Fanchiotti, and K. Steemers, eds., *Daylighting in Architecture: A European Reference Book* (London: James & James, 1993).

96. See, for example, D. Michael Utzinger and Pete S. Bochek, "Influence of Architectural Design on the Thermal Behavior of Atriums," in *Research & Design 85: Architectural Applications of Design and Technology Research: March 14–18, 1985, Los Angeles, California: General Proceedings* (Washington, DC: American Institute of Architects Foundation, 1985), 117–122; Mark Seymour, "Dynamic Designs on Atria," *Building Services* 14, no. 1 (January 1992): 27–29; Morad R. Atif, David E. Claridge, Lester L. Boyer, and Larry O. Degelman, "Atrium Buildings: Thermal Performance and Climatic Factors," *ASHRAE Transactions* 101, part 1 (1995): 454–460.

97. Å. Blomsterberg and M. Wall, "The Energy Impact of Ventilation and Air Infiltration in an Atrium," in *14th AIVC Conference: Energy Impact of Ventilation and Air Filtration: Proceedings* (Coventry, UK: Air Infiltration and Ventilation Centre, 1993), 42–49; Eino O. Kainlauri and Michael P. Vilmain, "Atrium Design Criteria Resulting from Comparative Studies of Atriums with Different Orientation and Complex Interfacing of Environmental Systems," *ASHRAE Transactions* 99, part 1 (1993): 1061–1069; "Atrium Research Will Improve Energy Savings and Indoor Environment," *Construction Innovation* 3, no. 4 (Summer 1998): 1–7. Two literature reviews provide analyses of the environmental performance of atrium buildings in Asia: Hiroshi Yoshino and Ken Aozasa, "Literature Survey on Thermal Environmental Strategies of Atrium Buildings in Japan," in *Proceedings of the Pan Pacific Symposium on Building and Urban Environmental Conditioning in Asia, Nagoya, Japan, March 1995*, ed. N. Nakahara (Nagoya: Organizing Committee of the Pan Pacific Symposium on Building and Urban Environmental Conditioning in Asia, 1995), 21–32; W. K. Chow and L. T. Wong, "Thermal Environment Design of Atria in the Hong Kong Special Administrative Region: A Survey Study," *Architectural Science Review* 42, no. 4 (1999): 235–252.

98. One of the most significant recent examples is the Federal Environment Agency building in Dessau, Germany, by Sauerbruch Hutton (2005), a sinuous, curving, low-rise building arranged around two atrium spaces.

99. See, for instance, Paul Walker's discussion of the environmental underpinnings of John Andrews's Intelsat Building. The competition jury that selected the building, and the commentators who reviewed it upon completion, largely assumed the architect's initial claims regarding performance to be true. Paul Walker, "Intelsat: Satellites, Science and Science Fiction," in *Historiographies of Technology and Architecture, Proceedings of the 35th Annual Conference of the Society of Architectural Historians of Australia and New Zealand. 4–7 July 2018 at the Faculty of Architecture and Design, Victoria University of Wellington, New Zealand*, ed. Michael Dudding, Christopher McDonald, and Joanna Merwood-Salisbury (Wellington: Society of Architectural Historians of Australia and New Zealand, 2018), 535–550.

CHAPTER 4

1. Francis Duffy, Colin Cave, and John Worthington, eds., *Planning Office Space* (London: Architectural Press, 1976), vi.

2. Amy Thomas, "Architectural Consulting in the Knowledge Economy: DEGW and the Orbit Report," *Journal of Architecture* 24, no. 7 (November 2019): 1020–1044.

3. DEGW would be a key consultant on Broadgate, which was developed by Rosehaugh Stanhope, the company Lipton set up after exiting Rosehaugh Greycoat Estates just prior to 1 Finsbury Avenue's completion. DEGW also completed several research reports for Rosehaugh Stanhope. See the review of Broadgate in Francis Duffy, "Building Critique: Broadgate," in Duffy, *The Changing Workplace* (London: Phaidon, 1992), 226–236.

4. Colin Davies and Hugh Pearman, "One Finsbury Avenue," *Designers' Journal* 6 (January 1985): 30. For a detailed history of the building, see Kenneth Powell, *1 Finsbury Avenue* (London: Lund Humphries, 2020).

5. Sutherland Lyall, "Commercial Success," *Building* 246, no. 27 (6 July 1984): 24.

6. Ian Latham, "Finsbury Finesse," *Building Design* 698 (13 July 1984): 18.

7. Davies and Pearman, "One Finsbury Avenue," 37.

8. Graham Ridout, "Good Connections," *Building* 250, no. 20 (16 May 1986): 46–47.

9. Martin Spring, "Trading Up," *Building* 262, no. 39 (3 October 1997): 76–80; Mick Brundle and Iain Lyall, "Warburg Dillon Read, 1 Finsbury Avenue, London," *Arup Journal* 35, no. 1 (2000): 15–19. On Arup's development of new sprinkler technology funded by Rosehaugh Stanhope Developments, see S. Peacock and R. Frost, "Active Protection for Atria," *Building Services* 13, no. 9 (September 1991): 32–35. On the energy, cooling, and servicing requirements of trading rooms in New York, see David Gissen, *Manhattan Atmospheres: Architecture, the Interior Environment, and Urban Crisis* (Minneapolis: University of Minnesota Press, 2014), 143–179. On flexibility in office development in London in this period, see Amy Thomas, "The Political Economy of Flexibility: Deregulation and the Transformation of Corporate Space in the Postwar City of London," in *Neoliberalism on the Ground: Architecture and Transformation from the 1960s to the Present*, ed. Kenny Cupers, Catharina Gabrielsson, and Helena Mattsson (Pittsburgh: University of Pittsburgh Press, 2020), 127–150. On the relationship between technology, building performance, and finance at Foster Associates' Hong Kong and Shanghai Bank building (Hong Kong, 1985), see Alexandra Quantrill, "The Value of Enclosure and the Business of Banking," *Grey Room* 71 (Spring 2018): 116–138.

10. See the discussion of the ORBIT Study in Thomas, "Architectural Consulting in the Knowledge Economy," 1030–1040. Thomas notes that Rosehaugh Greycoat Estates commissioned DEGW to assess the extent to which 1 Finsbury Avenue had adopted the

findings of the ORBIT Study. Though unacknowledged, the form and organizational diagram of the building was used as the architectural model in the handbook *Information Technology and Buildings: A Practical Guide for Designers* (London: Butler Cox, 1989), for which Duffy wrote the foreword. In a similar way to the ORBIT Study, this report was published by the IT consultancy Butler Cox with funding from AT&T (UK), British Telecom, Digital Equipment Company, and IBM (UK).

11. Thomas, "Architectural Consulting in the Knowledge Economy," 1038.

12. Thomas, "Architectural Consulting in the Knowledge Economy," 1022. On DEGW see also Thomas, "The Political Economy of Flexibility," 127–150.

13. Dean Hawkes and Richard MacCormac, "Office Form, Energy and Land Use," *RIBA Journal* 85, no. 6 (June 1978): 246–248.

14. Hawkes and MacCormac, "Office Form, Energy and Land Use," 247.

15. Francis Duffy, "Bürolandschaft," *Architectural Review* 135, no. 804 (February 1964): 148–154; Frank Duffy, *Office Landscaping: A New Approach to Office Planning* (London: Anbar, 1966).

16. Duffy, *The Changing Workplace*, 1.

17. Andreas Rumpfhuber, "The Incorporation of Dissent: Bürolandschaft's Legacy," *Harvard Design Magazine* 47 (2019): 89. See also Andreas Rumpfhuber, "In Praise of Cybernetics: Office Landscaping and the (Self-)Conditioning of Workers," *Footprint* 25 (Autumn/Winter 2019): 85–100.

18. Rumpfhuber, "The Incorporation of Dissent," 89.

19. In the English-speaking world, the figure of the knowledge worker had been theorized by Peter Drucker. For a discussion of the relationship between management theories and office organization, see Nikil Saval, *Cubed: A Secret History of the Workplace* (New York: Doubleday, 2014), 183–220.

20. Rumpfhuber, "The Incorporation of Dissent," 89.

21. Rumpfhuber, "The Incorporation of Dissent," 89.

22. See the account of the process given in Alfons Wankum, *Layout Planning in the Landscaped Office* (London: Anbar, 1969), 6–29.

23. Duffy, "Bürolandschaft," 154.

24. See Wankum, *Layout Planning in the Landscaped Office*, 19–24.

25. Duffy, *Office Landscaping*, 9.

26. Rumpfhuber, "The Incorporation of Dissent," 89.

27. J. M. Fraser quoted in Wankum, *Layout Planning in the Landscaped Office*, 5.

28. Eberhard Schnelle quoted in Rumpfhuber, "The Incorporation of Dissent," 89.

29. Rumpfhuber, "The Incorporation of Dissent," 88.

30. Duffy, *Office Landscaping*, 5.

31. It is worth noting, however, that Duffy's *Office Landscaping* contained a full bibliography, with abstracts, of the major publications on Bürolandschaft and office organization by figures who were part of, and associated with, the Quickborner team. This appeared to be driven by the publisher Anbar creating a subscriber base for such literature.

32. Juriaan van Meel, *The European Office: Office Design and National Context* (Rotterdam: 010 Publishers, 2000), 37–38. The German law of Codetermination was enacted in 1976, and the Swedish Work Environment Act became law in 1977. For an in-depth discussion of employee participation in planning in Sweden, and expectations regarding the provision of individual offices and group spaces, see Dennis Doxtater, *Architecture, Ritual Practice and Co-Determination in the Swedish Office* (Aldershot: Avebury, 1994), 101–121.

33. Francis Duffy, "Office Interiors and Organizations," PhD diss., Princeton University, 1974. A summary is published as Francis Duffy, "The Princeton Dissertation," in *The Changing Workplace*, 79–95.

34. Bevis Fuller, "Bürolandschaft: A Science of Office Design?," in Duffy, Cave, and Worthington, *Planning Office Space*, 61–67.

35. Francis Duffy and Colin Cave, "Bürolandschaft: An Appraisal," in Duffy, Cave, and Worthington, *Planning Office Space*, 70.

36. Francis Duffy, Colin Cave, and John Worthington, "The Principles of Office Design," in Duffy, Cave, and Worthington, *Planning Office Space*, 6–7.

37. Duffy, Cave, and Worthington, "The Principles of Office Design," 6.

38. Duffy and Cave, "Bürolandschaft: An Appraisal," 68.

39. Duffy and Cave, "Bürolandschaft: An Appraisal," 69.

40. Duffy, Cave, and Worthington, "The Principles of Office Design," 7.

41. Jose Manser, "Work, Rest and Play," *Designers' Journal* 42 (November 1988): 104.

42. Jan Carlzon quoted in Francis Duffy, "SAS Co-Operation," *Architectural Review* 185, no. 1105 (March 1989): 43.

43. Duffy, "SAS Co-Operation," 43.

44. Duffy, "SAS Co-Operation," 43–44. Duffy had explored these issues of status in a Princeton term paper, published as Francis Duffy, "Facing the Dilemma of Status," in *The Changing Workplace*, 24–36.

45. Duffy, "SAS Co-Operation," 43.

46. Duffy, "SAS Co-Operation," 46. See also the extended analysis of Swedish work culture and the role of the street in the SAS Headquarters in Doxtater, *Architecture, Ritual Practice and Co-Determination*, 139–142, 302–335.

47. Duffy, "SAS Co-Operation," 46.

48. Duffy, "SAS Co-Operation," 46.

49. Francis Duffy, "Office Cultures," *Architects' Journal* 195, no. 23 (10 June 1992): 28–39.

50. Martin Pawley, "The Ark's Architect and His Vision of Interaction," *Building* 256, no. 16 (19 April 1991): 22.

51. Matthew Coomber, "State of the Ark," *Building* 256, no. 9 (1 March 1991): 42; Dennis Sharp, "Erskine's Arc," *Building Design* 1039 (14 June 1991): 24.

52. Ralph Erskine quoted in Pawley, "The Ark's Architect and His Vision of Interaction," 22.

53. Pawley, "The Ark's Architect and His Vision of Interaction," 22.

54. Pamela Buxton, "Broadway Malyan Set to Rethink Erskine Ark," *Building Design* 1177 (17 June 1994): 1.

55. Deborah Singmaster, "Peopling the Ark," *Architects' Journal* 204, no. 16 (31 October 1996): 47–51.

56. Julia Cahill, "Turning the Ark into a Whole New Animal," *Estates Gazette* 618 (6 May 2006): 61.

57. Martin Spring, "The Incredible Hull," *Building* 273, no. 7 (22 February 2008): 52.

58. Duffy, "Office Cultures," 38.

59. Francis Duffy, "British Airways at Waterside: A New Model Office?," *Architectural Research Quarterly* 3, no. 2 (1999): 133.

60. Duffy, "British Airways at Waterside," 130.

61. Duffy, "British Airways at Waterside," 138. In an otherwise praiseworthy review of Waterside, Peter Davey considered these techniques and their architectural outcomes as "the embodiment of a power system every bit as frightening to individuals as that of the eighteenth-century oligarchy." Peter Davey, "The City in the Wilderness," *Architectural Review* 204, no. 1218 (August 1998), 42.

62. Duffy, "British Airways at Waterside," 138.

63. Duffy, "British Airways at Waterside," 135.

64. Duffy, "British Airways at Waterside," 138.

65. Duffy, "British Airways at Waterside," 139.

66. Duffy, "British Airways at Waterside," 139.

67. Duffy, "British Airways at Waterside," 139.

68. Compare Reinhold Martin's argument regarding the pervasiveness, by the mid-twentieth century, of an "organizational complex" that situated architecture within a broader patterning of life characterized in terms of modulated control: "And so techno-cratic and aesthetic research accelerated in the direction of ever more efficient mechanisms of *self*-regulation, *self*-organization. These in turn helped invent new kinds of cities, new kinds of architectures, and with them a new 'self,' none of which could be said to possess the traditional spatial properties that divided inside from outside in any meaningful sense." Reinhold Martin, *The Organizational Complex: Architecture, Media and Corporate Space* (Cambridge, MA: MIT Press, 2003), 7.

69. See Iain Borden's analysis of boundaries at the Broadgate development in Iain Borden, "Thick Edge: Architectural Boundaries in the Postmodern Metropolis," in *Intersections: Architectural Histories and Critical Theories*, ed. Iain Borden and Jane Rendell (London: Routledge, 2000), 226–235.

70. Gilles Deleuze, "Postscript on Control Societies," in *Negotiations*, trans. Martin Joughin (New York: Columbia University Press, 1997), 177–182.

71. Paolo Virno, *A Grammar of the Multitude* (New York: Semiotext(e): 2004). From a Marxist standpoint, this constituted capitalism's exploitation of workers' "'general intellect'—the diffused social knowledge of society." This capacity, which Marx thought was developed outside of conventional sites of work, was, however, subsumed by capital, which "puts to work the capacities to create and communicate that traverse social relations." What is known as real subsumption made subjectivity itself productive. Jason Read, "A Genealogy of Homo-Economicus: Neoliberalism and the Production of Subjectivity," *Foucault Studies*, no. 6 (February 2009): 33.

72. Michel Foucault, *The Birth of Biopolitics: Lectures at the Collège de France, 1978–1979*, trans. Graham Burchell (New York: Palgrave Macmillan, 2008), 226. On the passport structure at Waterside, see Duffy, "British Airways at Waterside," 138.

73. Deleuze, "Postscript on Control Societies," 179.

74. Compare the conclusions of Thomas, "The Political Economy of Flexibility," 145–147.

75. Foucault, *The Birth of Biopolitics*, 270–271.

Chapter 5

1. Dieter Kienast, "Interiorscaping or Pleasure in Verdure Planning Indoors," *Anthos* 28, no. 1 (1989): 28, 30.

2. Kienast, "Interiorscaping," 30.

3. For the US industry, see Danielle Narae Choi, "Risk and Fun: Dan Kiley's Interior Landscape for the Ford Foundation," *Studies in the History of Gardens and Designed Landscapes* 40, no. 2 (2020): 106; and David Gissen, *Manhattan Atmospheres: Architecture, the Interior Environment, and Urban Crisis* (Minneapolis: University of Minnesota Press, 2014), 102–103. For the UK and European industry, see Stephen Ashley, "Plant Control," *Building Services* 10, no. 12 (December 1988): 31; and Stephen Scrivens, "Analysis: Interior Landscaping," *Facilities* 2, no. 5 (May 1984): 6.

4. Ashley, "Plant Control," 35.

5. Richard L. Gaines, *Interior Plantscaping: Building Design for Interior Foliage Plants* (New York: Architectural Record Books, 1977); Stephen Scrivens, *Interior Planting in Large Buildings: A Handbook for Architects, Interior Designers, and Horticulturists* (London: Architectural Press, 1980).

6. Stephen Scrivens, "Interior Planting: Case Study 5. Alexander Howden House, London EC1," *Architects' Journal* 169, no. 11 (11 April 1979): 761–763; Stephen Scrivens, "Interior Planting: Case Study 6. Offices of Centraal Beheer Insurance Corporation at Apeldoorn, Holland," *Architects' Journal* 169, no. 17 (25 April 1979): 873–875; Stephen Scrivens, "Interior Planting: Case Study 13. Skyline Hotel, Adjacent to Heathrow Airport," *Architects' Journal* 169, no. 21 (23 May 1979): 1087–1088; Stephen Scrivens, "Interior Planting: Case Study 14. Worcester Square, Redditch, for Redditch Development Corporation," *Architects' Journal* 169, no. 23 (6 June 1979): 1167–1168. A further article analyzed a range of atrium buildings in Chicago: Stephen Scrivens, "Interior Planting: Case Study 15. Chicago," *Architects' Journal* 171, no. 5 (30 January 1980): 243–248.

7. On the development of plant physiology in the context of artificial environments, see David P. D. Munns, *Engineering the Environment: Phytotrons and the Quest for Climate Control in the Cold War* (Pittsburgh: University of Pittsburgh Press, 2017).

8. Compare the relationship between human and ecological systems in the Biosphere 2 experiment which ran through the early 1990s. See Tim Ivison, Julia Tcharfas, and Simon Sadler, "Biosphere 2's Experimental Life," in *Laboratory Lifestyles: The Construction of Scientific Fictions*, ed. Sandra Kaji-O'Grady, Chris L. Smith, and Russell Hughes (Cambridge, MA: MIT Press, 2018), 169–193.

9. Charles Rice, *The Emergence of the Interior: Architecture, Modernity, Domesticity* (London: Routledge, 2007), 2.

10. "A Great Space Taking Shape in New York," *Progressive Architecture* 45, no. 11 (November 1964): 196.

11. Choi, "Risk and Fun," 95–109.

12. Gissen, *Manhattan Atmospheres*, 71.

13. Choi, "Risk and Fun," 107; Gissen, *Manhattan Atmospheres*, 77.

14. Gissen, *Manhattan Atmospheres*, 67.

15. Roche discussed Fuller's proposal in relation to his own design for the United Nations Center, a development comprising a hotel and three forty-story office buildings opposite the UN General Assembly and one block north of the Ford Foundation. However, he played down his own ambitions relative to Fuller. Of the 500-foot-high atrium planned for the UN Center, Roche remarked to Museum of Modern Art curator Arthur Drexler, who was preparing an exhibition on Roche, Philip Johnson, and Paul Rudolph: "we are just doing a little skin around our little piece of the world." Quoted in Felicity Scott, *Outlaw Territories: Environments of Insecurity / Architectures of Counterinsurgency* (New York: Zone Books, 2016), 38. See also Boyer's discussion of the project's alignment of its cross axis with the entrance to the Ford Foundation building: M. Christine Boyer, "Reflections on a Glass," *Design Book Review*, no. 13 (Fall 1987): 37. The completed design included a much-reduced lobby structure linking two towers. See Eeva-Liisa Pelkonen, *Kevin Roche: Architecture as Environment* (New Haven: Yale University Press, 2011), 180.

16. Gissen, *Manhattan Atmospheres*, 82. As Gissen notes, however, there was never a stipulation in the code that these spaces should incorporate planting or gardens.

17. Scott, *Outlaw Territories*, 39.

18. Gissen, *Manhattan Atmospheres*, 84–97.

19. "A Great Space Taking Shape in New York," 194.

20. "A Great Space Taking Shape in New York," 196.

21. "Charity Begins at Home," *Progressive Architecture* 49, no. 2 (February 1968): 100.

22. "The New Headquarters for the Ford Foundation in New York," *Domus*, no. 462 (May 1968): 1. On these visual effects, see Scott, *Outlaw Territories*, 54–56.

23. Michael Sorkin, "The Garden in the Machine" (1987), in *Exquisite Corpse: Writing on Buildings, 1979–1989* (New York: Verso, 1991), 238.

24. Dan Graham and Robin Hurst, "Corporate Arcadias," *Artforum* 4 (December 1987): 72. On critiques of both Sorkin's and Graham and Hurst's position, see Gissen, *Manhattan Atmospheres*, 98–99; Choi, "Risk and Fun," 105.

25. Boyer, "Reflections on a Glass," 34–37.

26. Scott, *Outlaw Territories*, 60. On these themes see also Boyer, "Reflections on a Glass," 36.

27. Gissen, *Manhattan Atmospheres*, 79.

28. See Gissen, *Manhattan Atmospheres*, 77–81; Penny Sparke, *Nature Inside: Plants and Flowers in the Modern Interior* (New Haven: Yale University Press, 2020), 139.

29. Choi, "Risk and Fun," 95–99, 105–106.

30. See Munns, *Engineering the Environment*. On the most famous phytotron, the geodesic-domed Missouri Botanical Garden, or Climatron (1960), see Lydia Kallipoliti, *The Architecture of Closed Worlds, or, What Is the Power of Shit?* (Zurich: Lars Müller, 2018), 64–69; Danielle Narae Choi, "Outsiders," *Harvard Design Magazine* 47 (2019): 109–112.

31. Choi, "Risk and Fun," 98, 105; Gissen, *Manhattan Atmospheres*, 79.

32. Choi, "Risk and Fun," 100–105

33. Choi, "Risk and Fun," 109, fn 39.

34. Choi, "Risk and Fun," 98; Sparke, *Nature Inside*, 137.

35. Choi, "Risk and Fun," 103.

36. On the Ford Foundation's control of risk-based capital, see Scott, *Outlaw Territories*, 46–47.

37. Scott, *Outlaw Territories*, 60. Compare the detailed discussion of the role of the landscaped atrium of Arthur Erickson's Bank of Canada building in Ottawa (1979) in Maren Koehler, "Architecture as a Mediating Technology: The Bank Lobby in Post-War North America," PhD diss., University of Sydney, 2019, 185–245.

38. Kenneth Frampton, "A House of Ivy League Values," *Architectural Design* 38 (July 1968): 307.

39. Frampton, "A House of Ivy League Values," 307.

40. Frampton, "A House of Ivy League Values," 310.

41. Frampton, "A House of Ivy League Values," 307.

42. Frampton, "A House of Ivy League Values," 311. See Scott's discussion Frampton's position in Scott, *Outlaw Territories*, 60–61.

43. David Mellor notes that Centraal Beheer had "every incentive—and the help of government subsidy—to build the very best working environment, both to encourage existing staff to move and to help in the recruitment of new staff." David Mellor, "Hertzberger: The Centraal Beheer Office Complex, Apeldoorn," *Architectural Design* 44 (February 1974): 109. Interestingly, Kenneth Frampton chose to compare Centraal Beheer to Norman Foster's Willis Faber & Dumas Headquarters (1975) in Ipswich, United Kingdom, noting that they were both for insurance firms that had moved from a metropolitan center (London in the case of Willis Faber & Dumas) to a provincial town. See Kenneth Frampton, *A Genealogy of Modern Architecture: Comparative Critical Analysis of Built Form* (Zurich: Lars Müller, 2015), 166–183.

44. Francis Duffy, "Centraal Beheer Offices, Apeldoorn, Holland: Appraisal," *Architects' Journal* 162, no. 44 (29 October 1975): 899. On the building's city-like qualities, see Alan

Colquhoun, "Centraal Beheer," *Architecture Plus* 2, no. 5 (September 1974): 48–55; republished in Alan Colquhoun, *Essays in Architectural Criticism: Modern Architecture and Historical Change* (Cambridge, MA: MIT Press, 1981), 104–109.

45. Colquhoun, "Centraal Beheer," 50. See also Mellor, "Hertzberger: The Centraal Beheer Office Complex," 110; Duffy, "Centraal Beheer Offices," 903.

46. Colquhoun, "Centraal Beheer," 49.

47. See in particular the account of Duffy, "Centraal Beheer Offices," 898.

48. Graham Moss, "A Dutch Landscape," *Building Design* 267 (26 September 1975): 22.

49. Moss, "A Dutch Landscape," 23.

50. See Moss, "A Dutch Landscape," 23. Moss visited three years after the building was completed.

51. Colquhoun, "Centraal Beheer," 49.

52. Scrivens, "Interior Planting: Case Study 6," 874.

53. Scrivens, "Interior Planting: Case Study 6," 874.

54. Duffy, "Centraal Beheer Offices," 903.

55. Colquhoun, "Centraal Beheer," 54.

56. Jerzy Soltan et al., "Forum Discussion: 'Beyond the Modern Movement': A Conference Held at Harvard University, November 5, 1977," *Harvard Architecture Review* 1 (April 1980): 190.

57. Robert Stern, quoted in Soltan et al., "Forum Discussion: 'Beyond the Modern Movement,'" 216.

58. Peter Eisenman, quoted in Soltan et al., "Forum Discussion: 'Beyond the Modern Movement,'" 214.

59. Peter Eisenman, quoted in Soltan et al., "Forum Discussion: 'Beyond the Modern Movement,'" 214.

60. Robert Stern, quoted in Soltan et al., "Forum Discussion: 'Beyond the Modern Movement,'" 214.

61. Stanford Anderson, quoted in Soltan et al., "Forum Discussion: 'Beyond the Modern Movement,'" 215.

62. Terry Farrell, "TV-am Building," *Transactions of the Royal Institute of British Architects* 3 (1983): 100.

63. Dennis Sharp, "TV-am: The Other Story," *Building* 244, no. 7291 (13 May 1983): 41.

64. Terry Farrell, "Headquarters Building for TV-am," *A + U* 84, no. 2 (February 1984): 43.

65. Martin Pawley, "TV-am Fact and Fantasy," *Building Design* 643 (3 June 1983): 15; Farrell, "TV-am Building," 17.

66. The deal for the initial site identified for the project, in Wandsworth, fell through, though the date for the opening of the building did not change. Farrell and his development partner, Wiltshiers, had quickly to look for another site and secure development approval to keep the whole project on track. See Sutherland Lyall, "TV-am: Design-Build," *Building* 244, no. 7291 (13 May 1983): 44.

67. Lyall, "TV-am: Design-Build," 44.

68. Farrell, "TV-am Building," 104.

69. Farrell, "TV-am Building," 100.

70. Sharp, "TV-am: The Other Story," 43; Pawley, "TV-am Fact and Fantasy," 106; Farrell, "TV-am Building," 104.

71. Ian Jones, *Morning Glory: A History of British Breakfast Television* (Tiverton: Kelly Publications, 2004), 48–58.

72. Jones, *Morning Glory, 89.*

73. Jones, *Morning Glory*, 93–102. Jones suggests that Gyngell became Margaret Thatcher's favorite TV boss (95).

74. "TV interview for TV-am," transcript, Margaret Thatcher Foundation, online at https://www.margaretthatcher.org/document/105826, accessed 23 July 2022.

75. Leslie Martin and Lionel March, "Land Use and Built Forms," *Cambridge Research* 3 (April 1966): 8.

Epilogue

1. "A Hybrid Approach to Work," blog post, 5 May 2021, https://blog.google/inside-google/life-at-google/hybrid-approach-work/, accessed 30 July 2022.

2. Jonathan D. Solomon, "Helmut Jahn's James R. Thompson Center and the Aesthetics of Postmodern Citizenship," *Avery Review* 19 (November 2016), online at http://averyreview.com/issues/issue-19/aesthetics-of-postmodern-citizenship, accessed 6 August 2022.

3. Joanna Merwood-Salisbury, "This Is Not a Skyscraper," *AA Files* 75 (2017): 145–148. See the dossier of responses to the building in *Places* 3, no. 4 (1987).

4. Robert Benson, "The State of Space," *Inland Architect* 31, no. 2 (March/April 1987): 59–60.

5. Jim Murphy, "Panoply of Images," *Progressive Architecture* 62, no. 2 (February 1981): 97; Fulvio Irace, "Helmut Jahn: Building for the Community," *Domus*, no. 667 (December 1985): 22; Merwood-Salisbury, "This Is Not a Skyscraper," 145.

6. Michael Sorkin, "Palace for a Bureaucracy," *Connoisseur* 216 (May 1986): 35.

7. Sorkin, "Palace for a Bureaucracy," 36.

8. "The Building of the Year 2000," *Inland Architect* 24, no. 4 (May 1980): 9.

9. Helmut Jahn, "The State of the Art Building," *Inland Architect* 24, no. 4 (May 1980): 10.

10. Spes Mekus, "State Center's Interiors," *Inland Architect* 24, no. 4 (May 1980): 16–18. For the historical context of the integration of professional specialization in large-scale projects in Chicago, see Merwood-Salisbury, "This Is Not a Skyscraper," 143.

11. Minoru Takeyama, "The Catapult Which Will Fling Everybody into the Adventure," *A + U* 86, no. 1 (January 1986): 99.

12. Vladimir Bazjanac, "Energy Analysis [State of Illinois Center, Chicago]," *Progressive Architecture* 62, no. 2 (February 1981): 99.

13. Christopher Olson, "A Monument of Politicized Architecture," *Building Design and Construction* 26, no. 9 (September 1985): 60.

14. Jim Murphy, "2000 and Beyond: The New State of Illinois Center: Infamous, a Noble Effort, or Both?'," *Progressive Architecture* 66, no. 12 (December 1985): 73–75.

15. Lisa Goff, "Litigation against Murphy/Jahn," *Progressive Architecture* 68, no. 7 (July 1987): 25, 30; Mark Branch, "State of Illinois Center Update," *Progressive Architecture* 68, no. 11 (November 1987): 27.

16. Olson, "A Monument of Politicized Architecture," 60. See also Merwood-Salisbury, "This Is Not a Skyscraper," 145.

17. Steve Musal, "For Sale: Thompson Center, Slightly Used," *Medill Reports Chicago*, 13 October 2015, online at https://news.medill.northwestern.edu/chicago/for-sale-thompson-center-slightly-used/, accessed 30 July 2022.

18. Docomomo US/Chicago, "Re: James R. Thompson Center—Support for City of Chicago Landmark Designation," letter addressed to J. B. Pritzker, Governor of Illinois, 6 March 2019, online at https://docomomo-us.org/resource/files%2F421wifuyjueq0cjq.pdf, accessed 30 July 2022. A dossier on the preservation efforts is online at https://www.docomomo-us.org/register/james-r-thompson-center, accessed 30 July 2022. See also the nomination of the building by Landmarks Illinois to the National Register of Historic Places: Illinois Historic Sites Advisory Council, "RE: Thompson Center (State of Illinois Building)—Nomination to the National Register of Historic Places," 21 June 2021, online at http://www.landmarks.org/wp-content/uploads/2021/06/LI-Thompson-Center_National-Reg-nom-support-let_IHSAC_6-21-21.pdf, accessed 11 August 2022.

19. Richard Saxon, *Atrium Buildings: Development and Design* (London: Architectural Press, 1983), 1.

20. "Ford Foundation Building," Landmarks Preservation Commission Designation List 285, LP 1970, 21 October 1997, online at http://s-media.nyc.gov/agencies/lpc/lp/1970.pdf, accessed 9 August, 2022.

21. For a discussion of the new landscape design, see Danielle Narae Choi, "Risk and Fun: Dan Kiley's Interior Landscape for the Ford Foundation," *Studies in the History of Gardens and Designed Landscapes* 40, no. 2 (2020): 107.

22. See the full listing at Historic England: https://historicengland.org.uk/listing/the-list/list-entry/1422594?section=official-list-entry, accessed 9 August 2022.

23. The building was purchased by Dutch real estate development firm Certitudo Capital in 2015. See https://www.certitudo.com/en/certitudo-capital-designing-hertzberger-park-in-apeldoorn/, accessed 9 August 2022.

24. Jahn, "Thompson Center Inside Out," February 2020, n.p., online at https://cdn.vox-cdn.com/uploads/chorus_asset/file/19702654/2020_TC_INSDE_OUT.0.pdf, accessed 16 August 2022.

25. "Bringing Google to Chicago's Thompson Center," blog post, 27 July 2022, https://blog.google/inside-google/company-announcements/chicago-thompson-center/, accessed 30 July 2022.

26. As an organization overseeing its own extensive building programs, Google commissioned BIG and Heatherwick Studio to design the vast urban interior of its Bay View headquarters in California (2022), a building whose aim is to fuse environmental and organizational performance. See Danielle Abril, "Google's Campus Is Trying the Hardest, but Can Perks Compete with WFH?," *Washington Post*, 14 July 2022, online at https://www.washingtonpost.com/technology/2022/07/14/google-bay-view/, accessed 11 August 2022.

27. Compare Sylvia Lavin, *Architecture Itself and Other Postmodernization Effects* (Montreal: Canadian Centre for Architecture, 2020), 19–24.

28. Rem Koolhaas, "Paul S. Byard Memorial Lecture," in *Preservation Is Overtaking Us* (New York: Columbia Books on Architecture and the City, 2014), online at https://www.arch.columbia.edu/books/reader/6-preservation-is-overtaking-us, accessed 11 August 2022. See also Jorge Otero-Pailos, "Supplement to OMA's Preservation Manifesto," in *Preservation Is Overtaking Us.*

Index